STOP RANDOM ACTS OF MARKETING

STOP

RANDOM

ACTS OF

MARKETING

Deliberate & Practical Growth
Strategies for Mid-Market CEOs

KAREN HAYWARD

LIONCREST
PUBLISHING

STOP RANDOM ACTS OF MARKETING

Deliberate & Practical Growth Strategies for Mid-Market CEOs

ISBN   978-1-5445-0255-7 *Hardcover*

978-1-5445-0253-3 *Paperback*

978-1-5445-0254-0 *Ebook*

CONTENTS

———

INTRODUCTION

After working in the trenches within startups like CenterBeam, mid-market companies like Accelio, and large organizations like Xerox Canada, I turned my attention to working directly with mid-market CEOs. I have since had the privilege to speak to over five hundred CEOs—via Vistage talks, at the COO Alliance, and during one-on-one consultations. When I meet with small groups of CEOs, I begin each talk by listing out what I have found to be the top-ten growth challenges. They watch as I write the first few:

- *Stuck at a revenue number*
- *Not sure where to start*
- *Current customers are stalled*
- *Constrained by sales*

After I write each item, I turn to see the CEOs shaking their heads in recognition. I know they are well acquainted with these challenges.

As I continue, I ask everyone to weigh in. "Each CEO present can vote on five challenges that are most relevant to you," I begin, "but you should wait until I write out all ten." I already know they will all use one of their votes for the last item: *random acts of marketing.*

Invariably, that final item gets the most votes and, by far, the most laughs. When they see the statement, it resonates with them immediately, clearing the tension in the room. They see I understand. Now we can have a conversation about what is happening.

They know they cannot keep trying to pursue growth in a random way. Anything *random* is:

1. Made, done, happening, or chosen without method or conscious decision.
2. Lacking a definite plan, purpose, or pattern.
3. Without definite aim, direction, rule, or method.

To move ahead with clarity, they must first return to strategy.

START WITH STRATEGY

If you want to get somewhere, you don't get in your car and drive without a plan. The road could lead you anywhere. First, you have to establish where you want to go. Then you can execute on that plan. For that reason, we must start with strategy.

Many mid-market CEOs started their companies prior to the digital age. Others started within the past twenty years, during this age. No matter the case, they run fantastic companies today but often struggle to grow with the economy. Their companies are structured to deliver operational excellence, but they lack real growth strategies to accelerate revenue. They keep moving, trying to find the answer, but they often feel lost.

Over the last five years while working as a CMO-for-hire at Chief Outsiders, I have consulted with hundreds of CEOs and have seen firsthand that growing a company and running a company require different perspectives. Running a company is optimizing inside the four walls of the organization, driving efficiencies; growing a company is aligning to the forces outside the company—such as competitors, economic trends, technology evolution, and consumer expectations.

When I meet with CEOs one-on-one, they often share with me that they tried to hire a marketing agency, often for an exorbitant rate—hoping the agency would fix their problems. The challenge is that agencies are excellent partners to execute a well-thought-out plan and might even complement a growth strategy with a strong communications strategy, but they won't build growth strategies for the business.

What every CEO needs first is *a systematic roadmap* to grow their business. They need a clear plan for sustainable growth based on data and market insight.

This plan should then lead to execution. Now you have to actually get in the car and drive to get somewhere. In those same rooms filled with CEOs, I often ask, "How many of you have done a SWOT analysis—strengths, weaknesses, opportunities, and threats?" Everyone in the room will put up their hand. Then I'll say, "Now, how many of you have activated against it?" Maybe one person keeps their hand raised, if any.

What's going on here? They've checked off the box for SWOT. They've done what they were "supposed to do." However, they have not activated against the opportunities identified in the SWOT strategy in a meaningful way that gets them more business. In a dash for results, they have triggered activities and have bypassed the insights gathering and strategy steps.

Before you send out messages in advertising, at trade-shows, or in sales presentations, it is important that you know those messages will resonate with your target audience. The insights should inform strategy, and your strategy should deliver compelling results.

The systematic plan, or roadmap, I will encourage you to develop in this book is based on market insight and the voice of the customer. We'll look at best practices in both marketing and sales from *Fortune* 1,000 companies, which you can directly apply to your business. In the end, you'll be equipped to truly accelerate the growth of your company.

MARKETING AND SALES

Marketing and sales are both essential business drivers and should be built out of a clear strategy. I will argue that sales is the execution of a marketing strategy and hence a subset of marketing.

Here, it can be helpful to envision a fulcrum, with marketing on one side and sales on the other. In today's mid-market business-to-business (B2B) world, the end of the teeter-totter with sales is way up in the air. Where does that leave marketing? In the best-case scenarios, it is given some thought but is still not positioned optimally within the business. Mid-market CEOs have an immediate opportunity to bring this picture into balance.

From an investment perspective, most mid-market companies focus on sales as their main revenue lever. Naturally, they emphasize the importance of the sales cycle, which is a series of sales steps used to win business. However, if they want to win in a market where the power has shifted to the buyer, their focus needs to be on the "buyer's cycle" versus the "sales cycle."

Furthermore, because CEOs are so focused on operations, they can rely too much on sales to scale their businesses and often struggle to see the full picture. They need to look outside the window and understand the customer's point of view, market trends, and the competitive landscape. By knowing how the customer perceives their products or services and their competitors, and by understanding the buyer's options and how they actually go through the buying process, the mid-market CEO will realize the criticality of needing to first optimize marketing. Only then can they make their sales initiatives scale more effectively.

Recently, I was called in to help a $14 million environmental services firm that had been highly successful with past initiatives. They had recently launched an incredible new service, and they couldn't understand why they could secure only one customer. Even with a superstar sales leader and a highly talented sales organization, they were stuck. No matter how great they were or how many calls they made, the numbers wouldn't budge.

We did a deep dive and looked into the way the sales team was talking about this new service. The team walked me through the compelling features and benefits they would discuss with prospects. Soon, I saw what they were missing—something many mid-market companies surprisingly pass over—*the voice of the customer*.

They had not asked critical questions. What were customers concerned about? What were they looking for? How were they evaluating the service versus other options? How did they make their ultimate buying decision? Who were the stakeholders in the buying process, and what were they each concerned with?

As soon as we began the conversation with prospects who had chosen not to buy, we discovered that the sales team's messaging was confusing to them. Prospects couldn't gain a full picture of the service. They would say things like, "It doesn't do emergency response, so we couldn't consider it." Since the service offerings *did* include emergency response, we knew something was wrong. We needed to change the story being told and put what mattered most to customers front and center.

Within weeks of changing the messaging about the service, the sales force began to gain traction with their prospects. They went from telling a story that didn't resonate with potential customers to speaking on their level. The story being told was from the vendor's point of view—in terms they thought were compelling. They had too quickly skipped over the marketing side of their business; they had not taken the time to establish the right story and truly understand their competitive advantage. Once they did, everything else fell in line.

So why do most mid-market companies not focus first on strategically setting up their marketing first? Why do they keep moving full steam ahead, with most or all their focus on the sales force, while doing random acts of marketing? The answers to those questions are rooted in the way many of these companies began years ago.

When they launched their companies, marketing was fuzzy and less measurable. Companies scaled by growing sales forces and expanding channels of distribution. Prospects got all of their information from salespeople.

Today, prospects self-inform or conduct their research online prior to seeing a salesperson. *They* control the buying process and have access to full information. This digital transformation has significantly impacted the way prospects shop or choose vendors with whom they want to engage for further evaluation.

These companies' early focus on direct sales continues to impact the way they run to this day. They must step back from their traditional approach to growth, or else they will not be able to scale cost-effectively with how the marketplace operates today. I have seen this reality in my work time and time again.

MY EXPERIENCE AND LEARNING

For the first twenty years of my career, I moved between sales and marketing—starting as a sales rep and finishing as a VP of marketing. During a time when companies prided themselves on deploying best practices and training their employees, I went through every training available—from Xerox sales and quality training to astronaut training done through GE. I then took all that knowledge into the next ten years of my career, as I worked with mid-market and high-growth companies.

While working at Xerox, I held positions in HR/Operations and as a general manager, VP of sales, sales manager, and VP of marketing. Few executives go through sales, marketing, and HR like this. Because I was never siloed, I could see from all sides.

My experience has allowed me to gain a clear perspective of how a business can excel in our current time in history. I have seen the marketing end of the equation radically influenced by technology. People now find, research, and buy products and services differently than they ever have. In this book, I will show you how to be ready to respond to these changes.

Here, you have the opportunity to leverage my lessons from the trenches—to improve both the marketing and sales sides of your organization so that your company can grow and prosper efficiently. I will include several examples and lessons from my experience as a CMO and managing partner with Chief Outsiders, since this work has specifically focused on helping mid-market companies develop high-confidence growth plans to accelerate revenue.

WHAT TO EXPECT

As a mid-market CEO, you have all the same problems as larger companies without all the resources. Therefore, you must learn and practice the most efficient and cost-effective way to grow your company. This means you must develop a detailed plan. Then you must spend your money on what matters most for you and measure the ROI.

We will begin by examining the challenges you face today and the changes you need to make for tomorrow. Part 1 is all about gaining market insight and developing a real strategy using the voice of the customer.

We will then dive into actionable processes and tactics for marketing and sales that will allow you to achieve top-line growth. Part 2 focuses on implementing a marketing strategy. Part 3 focuses on execution in sales.

My hope is that you will be able to identify areas where you can step back and develop real and sustainable growth strategies so that you can execute against those strategies in deliberate ways. Let's get started with strategy.

PART I

START WITH STRATEGY

CHAPTER ONE

RECOGNIZE THE REALITIES TODAY

I recently spoke with a CEO who runs a $4 million software-as-a-service company. He couldn't understand why the company was stuck at a revenue number and could not grow. During our conversation, I realized that this technology company was not utilizing one of the most basic tech tools today: Google Analytics.

In fact, they had no way to measure website traffic or to see how they were performing against competitors online. The CEO could not see that he was missing out on easy wins, because he was still working from a "within the walls" perspective. His entire focus was on operations and the inside sales team.

Like so many mid-market CEOs today, he was losing

momentum and wasn't sure why. He couldn't step back and see outward to understand how technology has completely transformed the way his customers buy and how sales and marketing work today. Without understanding his digital footprint like all his competitors did, he was being left behind.

FROM AN INTERNAL FOCUS

I work with many CEOs who started up prior to the digital age. No matter the industry they are in, they initially experienced growth by relying on their sales team to call and develop relationships with large customers.

Many of these CEOs came from a finance or engineering background, and their focus was, naturally, operational. They wanted to run fast and rely on sales to do the rest.

When they started, that approach worked. The personal sales relationship mattered more than anything. In today's digital world, nobody wants to deal with a sales rep until they've researched the company, its offerings, and its reputation—including how well it's viewed by its employees. Potential customers look at all readily available data about the company before they'll ever agree to talk to a sales agent.

Companies that have traditionally relied solely on their

sales force to drive new business often struggle to adapt to a world in which anyone can access data about them at any time. The salesperson no longer holds all the information and educates the customer. In the digital age, the customer self-educates, eliminates most options themselves, and might reach out to the final three options for closer evaluation.

Today, salespeople engage more deeply in the sales funnel. They are no longer the first point of contact when a prospect reaches the point of consideration. Instead, it falls to marketing to create a cohesive, effective digital strategy that educates the prospect, drives enough interest and awareness, and answers enough questions about the company and its value to engage potential customers.

I have worked with so many CEOs who understand the importance of having a digital footprint but admit that they're still leaving some of the company's most important tasks to a junior marketing person. Somewhere along the way, someone in the company had suggested, "Maybe we need to have a blog. Maybe we should do some email marketing." So the CEO hired a junior resource to do all digital marketing and never took time to reconsider just how critical digital marketing is in the buying cycle today. This is a common but problematic scenario.

Below, you will find an illustration that shows how the

entire marketing and sales funnel has shifted from before the digital age to after.

THE NEW MARKETING AND SALES FUNNEL

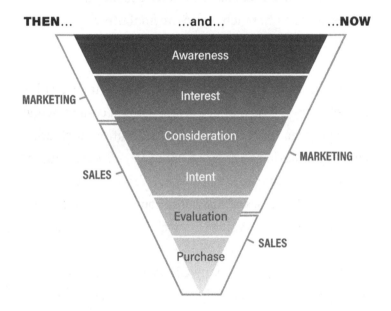

THEN... ...and... ...NOW

MARKETING

SALES

Awareness

Interest

Consideration

Intent

Evaluation

Purchase

MARKETING

SALES

THE WAKE-UP CALL

Some CEOs fail to place enough focus on marketing because they believe all they can measure is sales. They know that sales, like engineering, is measurable and that those within the field understand the metrics. Traditionally, marketing efforts were considered too vague to measure. How do you measure branding? How do you measure how much revenue comes directly or indirectly from an article in a publication?

While marketing may still not be as clearly measurable as sales, modern digital marketing is just as measurable, if not more measurable, than sales. If done correctly, you can have accountability and accurate metrics at every stage of the sales funnel.

Today's modern marketing and sales funnel is broken into three stages. The stages include top, middle, and bottom of funnel activities, which help you reach the right people where they are, move them through to become prospects, and ultimately turn them into customers who must be nurtured.

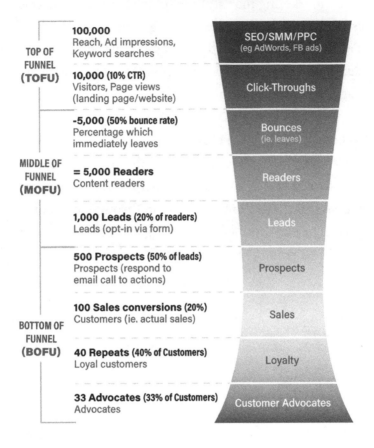

DIGITAL MARKETING FUNNEL (ANALYTICS)

TOP OF FUNNEL (TOFU)

100,000
Reach, Ad impressions, Keyword searches — SEO/SMM/PPC (eg AdWords, FB ads)

10,000 (10% CTR)
Visitors, Page views (landing page/website) — Click-Throughs

MIDDLE OF FUNNEL (MOFU)

-5,000 (50% bounce rate)
Percentage which immediately leaves — Bounces (ie. leaves)

= 5,000 Readers
Content readers — Readers

1,000 Leads (20% of readers)
Leads (opt-in via form) — Leads

500 Prospects (50% of leads)
Prospects (respond to email call to actions) — Prospects

BOTTOM OF FUNNEL (BOFU)

100 Sales conversions (20%)
Customers (ie. actual sales) — Sales

40 Repeats (40% of Customers)
Loyal customers — Loyalty

33 Advocates (33% of Customers)
Advocates — Customer Advocates

During a presentation I gave at the COO Alliance, I saw CEOs have moments of epiphany when they came to understand the reality of the new marketing and sales funnel today. I asked everyone to tell me what their key takeaway from the session was. One of the top executives there said, "Oh my gosh, we're not measuring anything in marketing." I responded, "Well, if you have absolutely no way to measure it, you probably shouldn't be doing it."

A company's marketing efforts need to be easily measurable, and today they can be. You can take advantage of the realities today, rather than run from them.

RESPOND TO HOW BUYERS BEHAVE TODAY

To recognize the realities today, sometimes it's helpful to make things personal. In my workshops, I'll often ask if anyone bought a car over a decade ago and if anyone bought a car within the past couple of years. I'll always have a couple of hands raised, and I'll ask each person to describe their buying process.

The person who bought a vehicle ten years ago invariably says that they talked to their friends, and thought about the car they wanted. Then they went to a range of dealerships and talked with sales reps, took test drives, and haggled on price and extra features.

The one who bought their car recently tells me they went online to Edmunds, TrueCar, or Cars.com. They'll describe their research process and the information they armed themselves with before they ever went near a dealership. Before they see the vehicle in person or meet a sales rep, the modern buyer already knows what color they want, the optional extras, all the specs, and how much they're willing to pay.

This is a clear picture of the shift that has taken place. Previously, the sales rep had all the power. Today, the well-informed customer does. Therefore, the buyer behaves much differently than they once did. This begs the question: Why are we not treating our customers any differently today?

UNDERSTANDING WHERE SALES AND MARKETING FIT

Although sales owns much less of the funnel today, sales execution is still critical. The problem is that companies rarely differentiate between marketing and sales or know where they fit in the big picture.

When many CEOs hear that marketing is more important today, they try to turn their VP of sales into a VP of sales and marketing. When someone is tasked with fulfilling both roles, particularly if that person is actually a salesperson, marketing is always put on the back burner.

Sales is a tough, all-consuming role. The head of sales has to ensure the cash register keeps on ringing, and has to focus on critical issues such as sales turnover and keeping their territories full. They will inevitably push marketing efforts to the next month or the next quarter. And once again, the junior resource gets tasked with all things digital.

It's surprising to see how few CEOs truly understand the difference between sales and marketing. At Chief Outsiders, where we serve CEOs and private equity firms, our most downloaded blog post is "What's the Difference between Sales and Marketing?"

One of the main purposes of this book is to bring clarity to this topic and to teach you which one to leverage and when. We'll tackle one at a time, and we'll begin with marketing, which is where you need to start today.

First, it's important to understand where you are and where you want to go—to gather market insight and to hear the voice of the customer so that you can build out your strategy in both marketing and sales.

CHAPTER TWO

GAIN INSIGHT FOR STRATEGY

———

In order to build a clear growth strategy, you must first have insight that informs your strategy. You can't keep moving fast if you don't know how people are responding to your product. You want a clear picture of both the market and your customer. Again, you need to keep looking outside your four walls.

While working at Xerox as their director of marketing for the printing systems group, my team and I identified a crucial need for a native data stream in order to effectively compete with IBM. It was the early '90s, and Xerox Corporation was excelling, selling high-speed, cut-sheet printers to big banks. Unlike the unwieldy 11 x 17-inch IBM fanfold printer outputs, Xerox machines could get all that data onto three-hole-punched 8.5 x 11-inch paper that would fit in a binder (which the bank's clients preferred, since it cost a lot less to mail).

This output was far more user-friendly. Xerox Corporation insisted on using a proprietary data stream converter to convert the data stream from the IBM mainframe to Xerox protocols for printing.

In Canada at that time, there just weren't that many deals to be had, so we had to win an extremely high proportion to keep moving forward. So we listened to our customers to gain an understanding about the market. They told us that they did not want a converted data stream, because whenever you convert data, it increases the risk of problems. Instead, they wanted our printing capabilities but with IBM's native data stream.

In response, my team built a front-end controller with our high-quality cut-sheet printing capabilities and the IBM data stream. It was so successful that it's now a multimillion-dollar business for Xerox Corporation globally. By looking outward, we identified how to properly leverage our competitive advantage. By gathering real market insight, we were able to go head-to-head with IBM and win.

MARKET INSIGHT

Market insight should inform strategy, which should drive execution. Before moving to execution in the second and third parts of this book, you need to understand how you're positioned in the market and how you're stacking up against the competition. You can start gaining valuable insight by using SWOT.

SWOT

By doing a SWOT analysis, you can more clearly see your strengths, weaknesses, opportunities, and threats. You can then activate against the insights you gain.

In my workshops, I split the leadership team into four groups and have each group work on one of the SWOT elements. I ask them to talk through what they think is working, how to improve their weaknesses, where they see opportunities, and how they can eliminate threats. I then rotate them so each group gets to work on every element.

I then take it a step further. Once the internal SWOT is complete, I ask the group to perform the same analysis on their main competitor. This kind of competitor analysis seems simple, but it's particularly illuminating and can clearly identify opportunities to grow into the strengths of other companies or to exploit their weaknesses.

I would encourage you to perform this kind of exercise with your own team. But don't stop with the exercise. You need to activate against your SWOT. It's often best to start with your strengths, although you may choose to first pursue an identified, time-sensitive opportunity or respond quickly to a weakness or threat. It all depends on what your SWOT analysis uncovered. Ask yourself: What is most important right now?

Elements of SWOT

Strengths: Many leaders identify their "people" as their strength. A colleague of mine always replies with, "Your strength is not your people unless all of your competitors are robots." You have to go deeper. What is it about your people that makes them your strength? For example, you might have the best engineers. So how can you leverage that strength? If you keep your engineers hidden from your customers, you are not showcasing your strength. How do you get your best engineers to engage with your best customers for the biggest growth opportunity? Perhaps you initiate a program that gets your largest high-growth clients working with your engineers. This would create a barrier for your competitors, too, because once your clients have a positive experience working with your best engineers, they won't want to move simply to save a few pennies.

Weaknesses: A high churn rate is a prime example of a weakness. An online cosmetic company I worked with had a churn rate of 15 percent. So every year, they had to sell 15 percent more than the last year just to backfill, which was a huge problem. It takes far more effort to open a new account than it does to renew or increase an existing account. To find the solution, you've got to establish why it's happening.

You might offer a survey to anyone who cancels their account or unsubscribes or to someone who fails to order for a month or more. You could even call the ten most recent losses and ask them why they're churning. Their feedback will be invaluable. You might find out that they'd go for longer-term contracts in exchange for a price break. Maybe your delivery times are too long, which is an operational problem you can easily fix. By listening beyond your four walls, you will know what you need to do from a product, service, or marketing perspective to activate against your weakness.

Opportunities: Market opportunities can result from many factors, including currency, economic trends, and technology shifts. For example, in a slowing market, you might put more of your resources into clients that are still growing. If the economy is predicted to grow more slowly and the aerospace industry is continuing to outpace the economy, then it would be wise to go more deeply into that vertical, thereby making market investments where you can get a better ROI.

Threats: When external factors could make you vulnerable, it's important to know how to respond. For example, if a major competitor has recently taken a significant capital infusion, you need to understand what actions are at your disposal to address the threat. You might move to longer contracts to solidify your key clients or implement a Focus Executive program (outlined later in the book) to drive higher and deeper client relationships.

MARKET POSITIONING

An important aspect of market insight is your market positioning. Where are you in the competitive landscape? How can you develop a strategy to win against key competition?

Market positioning comes from understanding yourself, your customers, and your competitors. Many companies struggle to position themselves effectively. A forensic laboratory I worked with was well equipped to handle complex, high-value, important cases, but because of their incorrect positioning and poor messaging, they were mainly approached for cheap, low-priority cases. They had not established themselves in the market correctly, so the market responded in kind.

Establishing your market position, your company's story, and your value proposition gives clarity about whom you serve and how you serve. It positions your business correctly and lets you attract more of the right kind of customers. Later in the book, we will explore how to execute your messaging effectively.

Your Market Characteristics

Understanding your market characteristics will help you further drill down your specific market positioning.

CenterBeam was a managed services provider and invented the first multi-tenant hosted exchange environment in the early 2000s. I was their VP of sales and marketing for seven years, then their CMO for the next four. In my early days at the company, we built the lead generation machine business with outbound calling and attacked multiple verticals.

Looking at the data, we found that we had a 17 percent lead rate with legal firms, but we could never close them. We used that insight to move away from pursuing legal firms and put those resources toward landing manufacturing clients, which we could close. We further established that CenterBeam was best targeted to highly distributed businesses with multiple office locations, narrowing our buyer persona further.

Over time, we developed these clear market characteristics:

- Midsize public companies for regulatory compliance
- Companies that have 100–2,000 PCs
- Businesses that historically underinvested in technology
- Highly distributed and had mobile workers
- Required outstanding end-user support in native English
- Cost-conscious companies

Market insight should lead to clear results. We relayed this information to the sales force so that they could direct their efforts to the right verticals. In turn, the company grew exponentially. This insight created our Ideal Customer Profile (ICP). Ultimately, CenterBeam had a successful exit when it was sold to EarthLink.

WHAT COMES NEXT?

I like to use the analogy that every CEO is flying a plane and has to keep building and improving the plane while it's in the air. Market insight can go a long way in helping you build your plan to be faster and go longer.

Before you make any changes to the plane, you want to know that those changes will give you the highest likelihood of success. With market insights, you can develop a solid marketing plan and ensure that your sales reps have everything they need to be productive, cost efficient, and successful

By having a strategy aligned with external analysis of the market and your key competitors, you improve your relevancy with customers and will be positioned for sustainable growth. Before moving onto executing your strategy, however, you must know how to follow the voice of the customer.

CHAPTER THREE

ABOVE ALL, PRIORITIZE THE VOICE OF THE CUSTOMER

If I had only one message to share with mid-market CEOs, it would be this: always prioritize the voice of the customer. When you do, your company will thrive. When you ignore the voice of the customer, you will lose your way and ultimately fail.

You cannot have effective marketing or sales strategies if they are not guided by the voice of the customer. However clever your strategy, if it isn't targeted specifically to the people you serve, it will go nowhere.

Early in my career at Xerox Canada, I learned this critical lesson through experience. When Xerox asked me to lead our PC program with a PC positioned as a word processor, I jumped at the opportunity to run a program. I put my head down and got right to work, learning the technology, training the salespeople, and garnering enthusiasm for my product line. About ninety days into my assignment, we had no traction, limited interest from our SMB target market as defined by HQ, and I was failing. Since failing was not an option, I decided to survey the market.

When I asked a dozen small business owners why they would buy a PC, every CEO answered, "To automate my accounting system." So I listened and responded. I made a deal with a local software provider, and we positioned our word processor as an accounting system bundled with accounting software. In little Montreal, we sold more than the rest of the country combined.

The lesson was clear: the voice of the customer will take you where you need to go. It will help you win early and often.

HOW TO CAPTURE THE VOICE OF THE CUSTOMER

You need effective ways to measure the voice of the customer to keep a pulse on why you're succeeding or why you're failing. If your business suddenly jumps from a 40 percent win rate to 70 percent, you need to understand what's driving that. If you can't close more than a few customers, you need to understand what's getting in the way.

There are different ways to get to the voice of the customer. Some methods are ongoing with core business processes, while others are more event based. Here, I will provide a few efficient options to capture this voice.

NET PROMOTER SCORE

Net Promoter Score, or NPS, is an ongoing measure that was developed by Fred Reichheld, a Bain Fellow, founder of Bain & Company's Loyalty Practice, and author of *The Ultimate Question*. NPS measures customer loyalty and was referenced in a *Harvard Business Review* article called "The One Number You Need to Grow Your Business." It's used by the world's biggest brands, such as Apple, Schwab, and American Express.

NPS measures customer loyalty based on a single question. It simply asks, "How likely are you to recommend ABC Company to a colleague?" Then the respondent answers with a score of 1 to 10 and can optionally offer notes about why they gave that score.

NPS is a cost-effective, strategic weapon in your marketing arsenal. You can use it to measure anything that impacts your customer. For example, you could measure for on-time delivery or customer satisfaction with the buying process. Once an order is complete, send them an NPS survey. The score itself is valuable, but it's the comments section that brings even greater insight.

As a CEO, it's hard to keep up with changing expectations of customers. This simple survey can help you pinpoint the opportunities that will give your business the most impact. You might gain great quotes from customers who loved your product, which you can publish elsewhere. You might reach out to these customers and ask them to post on social media. You'll also find people who didn't enjoy the experience. They'll raise issues that you may have been unaware of, and you can then easily remedy to improve the experience for future customers.

You can set NPS up internally, or you can contract a third-party service to do it for you. There are numerous companies that deliver the software as a service, and some offer a certain number of surveys free to get you started. Doing it internally can be a drain on your resources, so outsourcing it is a cost-effective alternative.

See Where You Stand

Satmetrix produces a yearly calendar of NPS benchmarks, outlining the average NPS by industry. For example, in 2018, the average NPS for financial services was 50, for airlines 44, for auto insurance 43, and for health insurance 13. For internet service providers (ISPs), the NPS in 2018 was -1. As you can see, scores fluctuate dramatically by industry.

JetBlue is the leader for airlines, with an NPS of 74. American Express leads the credit card industry, with an NPS of 60. Costco comes in first in the department and specialty stores category with an NPS of 79. For smartphones, Apple leads the category with a score of 60.

Find the benchmark NPS for your industry and see how you compare. Always aim to exceed that benchmark. Trend your scores, and then work to drive continuous improvement. For CEOs wanting an exit for their company, this is an important metric. Who is the leader in your category? That's the score you want to beat. It's all relative, so don't assume your NPS of 40 is bad without first looking at the other companies in your industry. The benchmark may be an NPS of 35, in which case, you're doing comparatively well.

Listen and Respond

At one point in my career, I moved from a company with a customer satisfaction rate of 99.9 percent to an ISP with an NPS of -27. The company with the high customer success rate rarely lost a customer, but the ISP had a customer churn rate of 20 percent.

It was quickly apparent that the ISP executives were not listening to the voice of their customers and therefore could not retain them. The company needed to use the feedback it got from customers to know how to improve. They needed to change their KPIs to reflect what customers actually cared about.

At another time, I was working with an environmental services company whose revenue was flat even though they ran incredibly hard. I discovered that, unbelievably, they'd failed to do any customer satisfaction monitoring. I moved to rectify this rapidly, using NPS. The company discovered they had a world-class score in the low 80s, even outstripping Apple, which scored 71 at the time. They had this incredible competitive advantage that they weren't leveraging with prospects or in their messaging, because they didn't know about it.

They also hadn't increased their pricing in several years, because they underestimated their worth. Discovering they had an NPS in the low 80s gave them the confidence to increase their pricing and, ultimately, drive incremental profitability.

BUYER PERSONA

Another way to understand your customer better on an ongoing basis is to build out a buyer persona.

Buyer personas are fictional, generalized representations of your ideal customers. Well-articulated and well researched personas help marketing, sales, product development, and innovation teams. Good personas can help you identify opportunities to differentiate your products or take friction out of your processes to streamline the customer experience. By relating to your ideal customer as a real human, you can internalize who they are.

Initially, you build a persona to discover what your customers are actually looking for. You want to understand their expectations, trigger events, and buying criteria. You also need to keep your buyer persona up to date, because expectations can change over time.

The comments gleaned from your NPS can feed into the buyer persona, helping you further refine the personality of your ideal customer. Once you know what's influencing your customers' buying decisions, you can alter your marketing messaging and communications to be super-relevant to your target audience.

When I work with mid-market companies and ask who their ideal customer is, the response is often, "We don't know. It could be anybody who wants a widget." But that's far too broad. There are segments where you'll have a high win rate and others where you'll experience a low win rate.

As you develop your buyer persona, you want to identify the three to five factors that this person uses to compare their purchasing options and make a decision. It will also help you answer a couple of key questions about your prospects. What are their perceived barriers to doing business with you? For example, a buyer might feel overwhelmed by the complexity of a product. What are their triggers? For example, a person who has experienced a breach in their cybersecurity is triggered to want to outsource cybersecurity going forward.

Buyer Personas by Adele Revella is a great book for helping you develop your buyer persona. If you want to learn more about building your ideal customer profile, this useful book is available on Amazon.

OUTSIDE CUSTOMER SURVEY

Finally, you can use an outside customer survey to capture the voice of your customer.

When working at CenterBeam, we believed that when customers called our help desk, they cared most about their calls getting answered within sixty seconds, as this had been traditionally identified as the most important metric. However, when we hired a customer research company to run surveys for us, they found that customers cared most that IT staff was able to resolve their issues quickly. Answering the phones fast was secondary.

The voice of our customer was loud and clear and led to simple changes within the company. We now knew it was better for us and our customers to staff our IT desk with level-two software engineers who could resolve problems quickly, rather than level-one engineers who could answer phones faster. We also demonstrated our value in our messaging by saying, "We focus on deeper expertise on our IT help desk, so we're able to resolve 80 percent of issues on the first call." The customers were willing to wait a little longer if they knew their issue was likely to be resolved once they were on the phone. Having level-two engineers on the first call became a unique differentiator versus our competitors.

A NOTE ON YOUR INTERNAL CUSTOMER

If you want true sustainable growth, you need to pay attention to the voice of not only your outside customers but also your "internal customers"—your employees. Today, your employees are stakeholders, so you need to think of them as internal customers. Do they like your offerings? How do they feel about the way the company is run? They are often an untapped wealth of insight and knowledge.

When I was at CenterBeam in the company's early days, our CEO, Kevin Francis, coined a new process and called it 3-3-3. This is a quick-and-easy, but powerful, way to incorporate the voice of the employee and identify issues and opportunities within your company.

We asked our employees to anonymously submit what they felt were the three greatest strengths of the company, the three biggest weaknesses, and the three things they'd do if they were the CEO. People jumped at the opportunity to provide feedback, and some wrote books. This kind of feedback is incredibly useful. Similar to SWOT, it allows you to leverage your strengths and respond to your weaknesses.

Some employees pointed out income disparities, which we evaluated transparently. Some pointed out tactical issues, while others focused on strategic efforts to improve product marketing and overall operations. We processed all this data, then created work groups where we actioned a huge number of their suggestions.

We kept the employees informed and implemented communications meetings at the departmental level, management level, and with a company newsletter. We also established an employee satisfaction measurement system that held managers accountable for the satisfaction of their teams.

I still use this powerful tool today as a consultant. It's highly effective, particularly with companies that are experiencing operational strife or those with a new leadership team trying to figure out where to focus first and who can benefit from early insights. We get ideas on products, company culture, and leadership. Sure, you'll get some responses that are simply self-serving such as, "Serve better lunches on a Friday," but over-all the feedback is exceptionally helpful—constructive and actionable.

Using this 3-3-3 method, you get a real response, without the filter of middle management, and because it's anonymous, respondents feel they can be more honest. As a CEO, you might gain important feedback about tools your people are using. At CenterBeam, employees raised issues about the customer service program. When the CEO went and sat with a customer success agent and saw it in action, he was astounded to see how frustrating and glitchy the program was. Middle management tends to filter the voice of the frontline employee, even though it's those frontline employees who interface with customers and are best placed to know where the issues are. When you realign executives with frontline employees, you get clarity.

MEASURING YOUR SUCCESS

To follow through on gaining insight for strategy, you need to have a clear way to measure how you're doing. Is your insight accurate? Do you know why you're winning in the market or why you're losing customers?

A few years ago, I worked with a Canadian cybersecurity company. The company was providing a sophisticated software as a service to mid-market companies so that they could better identify threats. When Dell entered the market with SecureWorks, a solution that was $15,000 a year cheaper, my client was thrown off guard.

The sales force rallied management, concerned by what they were hearing prospects tell them. "We're starting to lose more and more customers due to price," they said. From their perspective, price was the problem. It was all customers ever talked about. As a result, the company began to seriously consider a price reduction.

After working with them for a short time, I quickly identified the need to run a loss analysis. My client hadn't yet gone to the customers who chose Dell over them to find out more about why they made the choice they did. By interfacing with lost customers, we learned a lot about the way they actually viewed the two products side by side.

Most importantly, we learned that IT staff did not choose

my client because they didn't see them providing a well-articulated product roadmap; they were therefore perceived as a riskier solution. Dell, on the other hand, had a clear roadmap for going forward and staying abreast of the fast-moving world of cybersecurity threats. The clients never articulated the criticality of a solution roadmap to the sales force.

As our conversations continued, more came to the surface. The lost customers were, in fact, afraid of losing their jobs. They were reporting directly to CIOs, and they could not make the wrong choice on this solution. They had a low appetite for risk and were willing to choose a less fully featured product if they perceived it as safer in the long run. This was another example of where a persona would have helped both marketing and sales to execute more efficiently.

The insight we gained led to obvious solutions. The remedy was clear. My client could create a clear product roadmap and have their CTO do a video sharing their product roadmap and how they would continue evolving going forward.

Sales could have never identified this remedy because they could have never identified the core concern of customers. All they heard was, "We're choosing Dell because of price." That was the end of the conversation, as it is in so many organizations.

According to win-loss specialists, the fact is that in the sale of any kind of technology, price is the deciding factor for customers less than 15 percent of the time.[1] Customers look at so many other factors first: the product itself, the professionalism of the sales rep, the follow-up they receive, and more.

In this scenario, we had one key finding, but we also benefited by learning about more issues customers were facing in their path to choosing a solution. For example, one prospect said, "You took such a long time to follow up with me." The sales rep went back to his log, confused. He had followed up within twenty-four hours. Soon enough, my client identified a glitch in the marketing automation technology that was misdirecting leads, causing significant delays in the sales reps' ability to follow up. Again, there was an easy remedy, but the company needed a clear way to get visibility to the problem.

WIN-LOSS ANALYSIS

As seen through this example, a critical way to measure your success is through a win-loss review. Once or twice a year, take a sample of your most recent wins and losses. Set up a call flow and use an independent third

---

1   Beacon Worldwide, "Win/Loss Analysis—A Different Approach," accessed August 30, 2019, https://beaconworldwide.com/sales-enablement-services/win-loss-feedback/.

party so that the customers feel comfortable being honest and open.

Ask for feedback. Why did they ultimately decide to choose you (or not)? How did the opportunity emerge and evolve? Who else was involved in the buying process and how? With these answers, you can map your collateral and sales processes. You can also ask about features and pricing. Ask about how much impact pricing and features had on the customer's decision. In this process, you learn about your competitors and find out why and how they are winning.

If you conduct ten of these calls with each won or lost opportunity, you'll get invaluable feedback that can help drive success.

DIGGING DEEPER

Ken Allred of Primary Intelligence, who deals exclusively in win-loss analyses, said that salespeople see only the tip of the iceberg, so it's dangerous to base company insights and their idea of the voice of the customer on anecdotes from the sales teams.

Imagine you're a purchaser. You've gone through a sales process, during which time you've talked to two sales-people, made your buying choice, and opted for the less expensive product. Then a sales rep from the losing company phones up and asks you why they didn't win. As a purchaser, you will most likely tell them something short and simple to get off the call, so you'll tell them your choice was based on cost.

However, if you were to dig deeper and find out how the purchaser went through the process of selecting a product, you would usually find the real reason is something else entirely—perhaps perceived value, warranties, references, or the lack of professionalism of the sales process.

To use a consultant or win-loss service company with trained interviewers, you (or the CEO of your company) should send lost customers a simple email, thanking them for their consideration and letting them know about a specific person who has been hired to identify opportunities for continuous improvement and growth. In the email, you ask whether they would be open to talk to this individual for thirty minutes to give some frank and honest feedback to help the business improve.

You might be surprised by how many people are willing to give feedback. As mentioned, I have personally worked on the interviewing side. I ask lost customers all kinds of questions about their buying journey, starting with how their need arose, where they went to research, what factors they prioritized, and how many other companies they considered. I don't try to resell to them or extoll the virtues of the company they didn't choose, but instead, I make it clear we value their honest feedback. The insights companies gain through my open conversations with lost customers are priceless.

MEASURE WHAT'S IMPORTANT TO YOU

To measure effectively, you need to know what you want to measure and why. What are you going to do with the results? How are you going to act on the outcome? Answer these questions and then pursue the measurements that matter most to you.

As we discussed in the last chapter, you need to have a way to pull information and feedback from your customer base on a regular basis. You might measure how your customer service team is performing by sending a survey to customers that asks, "On a scale of one to ten, how professional was our customer service agent?" or "Did you get an answer in a timely fashion?" If you get low scores, do a root cause analysis, and find out why that happened. Then figure out how to fix it. Make sure to close the loop with the customer.

You can perform these types of measurements in many parts of your business. You might want to track the effectiveness of your sales process. You could do this by pulling data on close rates. See the digital marketing funnel graphic for a set of complete metrics to measure.

You might want to see how you're doing on the product development side. Contact customers who have had your product for a year or more, and ask them how it's working out. In turn, they might give you a few innovation ideas—what new features or improvements they'd like to see in the next product generation.

ARE YOU READY?

Now you recognize the realities of the buyer journey today. You have put in time to gain market insight and to understand the voice of your customer.

You are set up for success. You are ready to activate against your strategy and implement marketing and sales efforts.

PART II

MARKETING EXECUTION FOR GROWTH

CHAPTER FOUR

START WITH SEGMENTATION

When it comes to marketing execution, segmentation is an ideal place to start because it allows you to know where to place your focus in your marketing.

By segmenting your client database, you gain a clearer picture of how much business you're getting, where you might be able to find more customers, or where you might be taking advantage of the customers you have. Ultimately, segmenting should help you determine where to put resources to engage with different segments in the market or different segments of your customers.

Our work with a franchise owner of an indoor sports venue demonstrated the importance of segmenting. Together, we discovered that the CEO was shooting in the dark, doing random acts of marketing, because he had not taken time to segment his prospective market.

He was the first franchisee in his region. Business was doing well until competitors began to spring up. In the early days, his business was a new concept in the area, so he experienced rapid growth. But eventually, his main park suddenly had three major competitors within a twenty-minute drive, giving consumers more choice, and presenting him with significant revenue challenges, until he ultimately experienced a 20 percent revenue decline.

So the CEO tried everything and anything. He tried monthly email blasts. He hired a social media agency and a marketing agency. When nothing worked, Chief Outsiders was brought in to help. We listened to the voice of the customer, and our CMO completed a comprehensive analysis of the competition. We discovered that each location had unique needs, and we quickly identified what needed to happen inside and outside of the company to turn things around.

Instead of trying a one-size-fits-all approach, we worked with each of the four distinct markets and came up with unique plans for each. We used demographic segmentation to great effect. We looked at the location of each park and the demographics of those who lived there. For example, in a neighborhood with a school or lots of children, we'd put a heavy emphasis on birthday-party business outreach. Each of the four plans was geared toward gaining new customers, regaining lost customers, and increasing visits of existing customers.

We used this segmentation to establish what to focus on, and now the CEO knew where he could compete with particular product offerings and how to give each local population exactly what they wanted.

Our efforts were hugely successful. With our help, the company went from losing 20 percent a year to seeing an 18 percent increase in just five months.

FIRST SEGMENT YOUR DATABASE

In order to know where to place your marketing efforts, you can start by segmenting your current database. This segmentation will give you insights into where you're already winning and losing. You can take this information into your marketing strategy.

There are many ways to segment your customer database, including geographic, demographic, and behavioral segmentation. In the previous example, we used both geographic and behavioral segmentation. Geographic segmentation involves looking at where the majority of your customers are located and where your most profitable customers are. Behavioral segmentation is based on actual consumer buying behavior.

One way to segment your current customers is to look at churn. Look at their profile and their size, then look at their churn rate. Pinpoint those customers who are coming in and leaving, and identify them. You can use this information to stop targeting customers who meet this profile, and look instead to the profiles of those customers who stay the course and drive the highest client lifetime value.

THE FOUR QUADRANTS

A helpful way to segment is to place your customers into four quadrants. The following graph is taken from Chief Outsiders' *Growth Gears* book. The graph has an X and Y axis. On the Y axis, you list your customers in terms of revenue or profit, then along the X axis, you add in their growth potential.

CUSTOMER DEVELOPMENT STRATEGY

For the customers in the lower left corner—your lowest-profit clients who are also those with the least room to grow—you'll most likely need to instigate a price increase and possibly fire some of them. There are many ways to fire customers without causing them to leave bad reviews. You could stagger multiple price increases targeted only to this group within a year, and you'll see a number of them leave of their own accord. You can also be honest with them and explain that their customer support usage far exceeds the revenue, so they may be better served at a different business. A common option is to implement a price increase to drive profitability for that customer segment.

Rafi Mohammed, a pricing guru, wrote *The 1% Windfall*, in which he advises using small, incremental pricing tweaks to drive outsized returns. His premise is that a large company can roll out a 1 percent price increase and see, on average, an 11 percent gain in operating profits. Few customers will leave a product or service they are happy with for a 1 percent price rise, and many won't even notice.

The upper-left quadrant is for those customers whom you want to maintain, so you'll need a maintenance strategy for mid-level customers.

The lower-right quadrant is reserved for customers whom you identify as those with potential that you'd like to put a growth plan in place for. For the growth-potential group, consider a competitive replacement strategy that both your marketing and sales teams can carry out. When I was at Xerox, the sales team would get a competitive replacement bonus each quarter. For every Canon 400 we replaced with a Xerox machine, we'd get a time-limited bonus spiff to drive urgency. To equip us with everything we needed to make that happen, we'd receive training in the old product's limitations and in the Xerox machines that could outperform it.

In the upper-right quadrant—customers who bring you the biggest profit and have the greatest room for growth—would fall into the platinum customer group. For members of this special group, you'll want to provide white-glove service. For example, you might create a dedicated phone line that takes them straight to your most senior reps and gives them easy access to your top engineers. You want to do everything you can to retain these customers and maximize the opportunity there. At CenterBeam, all the top-revenue clients were assigned an executive from the leadership team who would regularly review their accounts and keep in touch quarterly with the senior leadership at the company. Be sure to tell them they are your very best clients!

For this final group, take what you learned from your SWOT analysis. Leverage your strengths to maximize satisfaction with your platinum customers. If your strength is reporting, for example, you could ask your platinum group how they use your current reporting and what additional reporting features or capabilities they'd like to see. Or perhaps your problem-solving is your key strength, and you could leverage that by creating a solution or product that addresses a particular issue or pain point your platinum customers may face, thus increasing your value.

Many companies treat all of their customers equally, even though some are clearly more valuable than others. If customers don't add much value but regularly consume your time or resources, you need to take action. By implementing a simple price increase, you will set yourself up to pursue larger, higher-profit clients. Your price increase actually becomes part of your positioning.

PRICING

When you segment your database, also take time to segment by price. In *Pricing with Confidence*, Reed Holden describes a revealing method of plotting all of your customers on a graph with their current pricing on the X axis and volume on the Y axis. It provides a visual representation of customer pricing, and it can reveal some surprising insights.

You might find, for example, that customers who are better at negotiating are paying significantly less than customers who are not good negotiators. You can then step back and consider if this should be the case. Should the former segment pay less simply because they knew how to haggle?

USE THE DATA YOU GAIN FOR STRATEGY

You can be creative in your segmenting. Your X axis could reflect industry growth instead of profit potential, for example. The point is to be able to both leverage opportunities in your customer base and identify areas in which to focus more resources when looking for new customers of high-growth segments or cross-sell opportunities.

Imagine you segment your current customers by industry and find that you're getting the most traction from the financial services and manufacturing sectors. Now you can focus your marketing efforts on those sectors.

You can take the data one step further and get a market research report from IBISWorld, which shows you all the key trends and latest happenings in your identified industries. In the report, you might see that manufacturing is going to grow by 5 percent while financial services is going to shrink and consolidate by 1 percent. You can then place more of your resources on the new customers in manufacturing. This is affordable, comprehensive secondary market research and is readily available for your industry or those of your target segments.

MESSAGING

As you gain insight into where your biggest opportunities are, you can better hone your messaging to speak to your current customers and attract the right new customers.

You build lasting relationships with current customers through effective, targeted communication. You also reach more ideal customers through the right messaging in all of your external communication, which we'll discuss in the next chapter.

CHAPTER FIVE

YOUR MESSAGING

I have received many calls from CEOs who tell me they are going to do a new website. When I ask them why they want a new website, they tell me, "Well, we just do. It's old. It's tired." But they miss the key issue—a website is the end result of a communications strategy, and it's only one channel of communication.

So many companies dive into creating a brand-new website without having any kind of strategy, plan, or goal in place to help guide them, so the messaging, targeting, and brand voice are all over the place. Ultimately, the website doesn't do what the business hoped, because a website in itself is not the golden ticket of marketing.

THE RIGHT MESSAGING

To get the messaging right, you want to magnify your

strengths and use the customer insights you've gained. Look at your sales history. Establish who your competitors are and your main opportunities for growth. You'll use all of this to build your brand house, also known as your messaging platform, from the foundation up.

Turn all your learnings into succinct, clear statements, values, and ideas that you can leverage across multiple communications channels. Your messaging should show up on relevant social media, on your website, and on any other channel your target prospects dial in to.

Remember, it doesn't matter what *you* think is important; all that matters is what your *customers* think is important. Think back to the example I gave from CenterBeam. We thought answering the phones in less than sixty seconds was critical, and we used this as one of our key messaging points. But we discovered, through research, that our customers didn't care about that. They wanted us to be able to resolve their problem when we did answer the phone, even if it took a little longer to make contact. So we changed our messaging to include what our customers wanted—level-two engineers who could solve problems. This was what set us apart from our competitors.

VALUE PROPOSITION

Before you jump into working on any single messaging

channel, you need to take a step back and figure out exactly what your value proposition is.

In the previous example, we found our value proposition by hiring an outside company to survey customers. You could start by interviewing ten customers on your own to find out what really matters to them. Then look at your competitors, and establish how you can position yourself against them. Which strengths make you different? Hubspot defines your value proposition as your unique identifier.[2] Without it, people don't have a reason to work with you over somebody else.

Use all of this information to make a clear, concise statement of the things that matter to your target market.

When Chief Outsiders was contracted by Forensic Analytical Sciences, we took an in-depth look at their messaging. We found that they consistently talked about three things: synthesis, their services, and their laboratory. They could easily see those elements as part of their value proposition. However, they failed to articulate that they were specialists in complex cases. When it really matters, Forensic Analytical Sciences is the go-to lab. We encouraged them to clearly communicate their positioning in

2   Lindsay Kolowich, "How to Write a Great Value Proposition," Hubspot, June 5, 2018, https://blog.hubspot.com/marketing/write-value-proposition.

their value proposition. In fact, we insisted that all their messaging flow from this point.

MESSAGING FRAMEWORK

A Google search of "messaging templates" will bring up several different options and examples. Below is an example of a messaging framework that is straightforward and easy to use. Use the framework as a guide for all of your messaging.

Even if you hire a marketing agency, they will have a difficult time achieving significant results without first having your messaging framework. I'll review below the elements to focus on here.

TARGET BUYERS
CFOs, CEOs, Controllers

DECISION MAKER
CFO, CEO, Controller in some organizations who need to streamline their ERP reporting process

POSITIONING STATEMENT
We leverage your ERP to the fullest, making your reporting processes clear, easy, and quick. This enables highly efficient, real-time financial and adhoc reporting with live data refresh and drilldown directly from your ERP with little to no IT support.

KEY MESSAGE 1	KEY MESSAGE 2	KEY MESSAGE 3
Enterprise software for budgeting, reporting, BI, and financial close management that is built to operate within MS Excel with full Excel functionality.	Engineered to scale to provide fast reporting functionality to thousands of users across large networks.	Lightweight platform that works within key internal controls and allows you to make sense of the numbers and gain control over your ERP.
PROOF POINT 1	**PROOF POINT 2**	**PROOF POINT 3**
Support for Key Message 1	A typical installation with a single reporting server can provide fast reporting results for 300 users running 8000 reports a day.	Support for Key Message 3

VALUE PROPOSITION
ABC Company puts your information right at your fingertips, helping you manage your business better and more efficiently with timely, accurate information.

COPY BLOCKS
Longer 25, 50, and 100 word descriptions of your offering and organization.

First, you want to answer: Who is your target segment? What are the job titles of your primary target and sub-targets? Once you answer these questions, write your positioning statement that clearly defines what position you want to take in the marketplace.

Next, you need to come up with three key messages, followed by proof points—these support your messages. Proof point number one supports key message number one and so on. Proof points could be testimonials, proven results for previous customers, or industry awards—anything that gives credibility and believability to the messages they support.

Finally, you have your value proposition followed by copy blocks. Use twenty-five-, fifty-, and hundred-word descriptions of your organization and services. You'll use these over and over. This is your foundation, your messaging framework.

HORIZONTAL OR VERTICAL MESSAGING

Now that we've discussed messaging, it's time to discuss whom to share that messaging with. Are you going for horizontal or vertical messaging, or both?

You need to consider how specific you want to get. Do you speak globally to the industry? This is known as horizontal messaging. Or do you target certain demographics or industries? This is segment, or vertical, messaging.

Sometimes you can take a horizontal platform and present it in vertical terms. For example, CRM maker Siebel created a horizontal platform first. They became the number-one software provider in the CRM space and were eventually acquired by Oracle. They then took one vertical at a time, creating industry teams and configuring that platform to be specific to the subset in the industry they were targeting. They made each edition of their platform sector-specific by using the relevant industry terminology. Their carefully chosen words convinced prospects that Siebel understood their industry.

Selling outsourced IT services at CenterBeam, we were serving a not-for-profit vertical sector, and when speaking to these companies we had different messaging than when dealing with for-profits. When we talked to nonprofits, we'd express that we understood the importance of their mission and that we were keen to support their sector. We'd even offer their twelfth month free for them as a way of giving back and supporting not-for-profits.

When we were selling to healthcare companies, we'd explain our security features and how we could help with HIPAA compliance. Although we were selling the same service, we emphasized different features according to the industry of the prospect we were targeting.

We also had to learn what messaging worked by validating it. One of our initial messages was that our service worked remotely. We supported people all over the world, so a prospect needn't worry about our ability to support their clients in five separate locations. This was a great horizontal message about our ability to support remote users, but it didn't resonate with our target audiences, because they weren't necessarily all over the world. The message positioned us as a global provider, and the prospects perceived we were too big for them. We were able to easily adjust the messaging for our audience.

When moving into a new industry, you need to understand what challenges and opportunities are present within it. If you're targeting the healthcare industry in your messaging, you need to know that these companies are trying to deliver better patient outcomes. If you can succinctly demonstrate how your product helps them achieve that goal or priority, you'll position yourself as more interesting than more generic competitors. Use the language they use within their industry to connect with them on a meaningful level.

BREAKING INTO VERTICALS

Every business leader (in B2B) or customer (in B2C) wants to know whether your product or service is relevant to them. The easiest way to reassure them is to speak with authority and insight into their industry, which builds trust and encourages them to continue to engage. When deploying vertical messaging, use comparisons and talk about clients you work with as proof points.

If you are a young company looking to break into a new vertical, you might not have industry-specific proof points to offer prospects. Both marketing and sales need to know how to talk about the industry with as much insight as possible. You want to approach each vertical as specifically as possible. IBISWorld's US Industry Reports and Global Trends reports can provide the needed insights.

A company may serve four or five key verticals, but their products and services may still be relevant to many others. In the case of the crime lab, they were targeting lawyers or people who require DNA analysis. They used horizontal messaging even though they have a specific service that's useful to many sectors. As long as you have a core message, you can then refine it for a specific vertical.

Once you've developed your message, you'll want to carefully consider how to share your message across the channels that are most relevant to your audience. We'll explore this omni-channel approach to marketing in the next chapter.

CHAPTER SIX

AN OMNI-CHANNEL APPROACH

Once you know the key aspects of your messaging and whom you want to target, it's time to share what you have to say through an omni-channel approach to marketing. While your messaging should be consistent across channels, you want to share it in unique, creative ways on each channel. For example, you might post a video on Facebook, while you write a longer blog post about the same topic on your website.

Here, we'll look at a few important "channels" where your messaging should be clearly conveyed.

WEBSITE

If you want to have a good website, you certainly need

to get the messaging, or content, right. But in order for users to care about what you have to say on your website, the design and navigation can't get in the way.

Start with design. If your website needs to be updated, invest time and money to make sure visitors won't click away simply because the site looks old or isn't visually appealing. Keep in mind that excellent design will only go so far if the site is confusing to use. Navigation is just as important to user experience.

NAVIGATION

Navigation refers to how your website is laid out, and there's real skill involved in perfecting it. For example, if you want different messages by industry, you should have industries as a top navigation item. However, if you market by product, you'll want to use products as the top navigation items.

Clear navigation is important for optimized user experience and for Google crawlers. A sitemap is also beneficial for Google indexing and helps your readers find their way around your site. You also need to be easy to contact, so make sure you have a clearly visible Contact Us option on your home page.

CONTENT

Once you spend time on good design and clear navigation, you need to ensure that your content is strong. What do you want people to do on your website, and how can you support them as they research and shop? To answer these questions, you have to think from a customer standpoint. When they research your product category or service, what questions do they ask, and how do you answer those questions? By asking your salespeople what the top-ten objections are, you can have an easy starting place for content.

If pricing is the most critical perceived barrier, consider using a pricing calculator that walks a client through their current costs, then shows them the cost of your service and the price difference. If trust is a common objection, you need to answer why a brand-new customer should trust you through your content. For example, you could feature testimonials from current customers to showcase the quality and trustworthiness of your product offerings.

The content on your home page is key. When you land on a home page, you should be able to quickly identify what that company does, whom they serve, their market position, and why they are different. In the case of the forensics laboratory, their original home page simply didn't showcase their strengths. Their headline mentioned "the care your case deserves," and they mentioned synthesis, services, and laboratory. But for new visitors, it was incredibly challenging to understand what they did and whom they did it for.

Chief Outsiders first advised they change the name of their company to Forensic Analytical Crime Lab, because it tells people what the company is. Then we designed a DNA-based logo. In the messaging, we established market position by outlining that this was a crime lab for complex cases. Rather than have a wall of text filled with technical jargon, the message on the home page changed to "Forensic Analytical Crime Lab distinguishes itself with expertise in multiple disciplines. Your case will be reviewed by one or more experts in DNA, criminalistics and/or pathology for the complete story."

Blogging also comes under content. Your blog should support the reader on their buying journey, as they research the product or service and ask questions. Google will reward you for having fresh, relevant content. Yes, you can pay for search engine advertisements, but organic ranking is free, so you should make the most of it. When a subject-matter expert can more efficiently explain their answers on video than they can in writing, a video blog is an excellent option. Pick the top questions you are asked, and work with the subject-matter expert to create a series of short videos.

Throughout your website, you want to give your customers lots of opportunities to engage with you. Make sure you utilize impactful, well-placed calls to action, or CTAs. CTAs should include enough information to persuade the user to take the next step. Examples include the following:

- Sign up for a free consultation or a newsletter
- Download an e-book
- Register for a podcast or a webinar
- Watch a video

VISUALS

Photographs are also invaluable messaging tools and should underpin the concept of what you do and whom you serve. People like to know whom they're doing business with, so it's a good idea to have pictures of your leadership team somewhere on your site as well.

The forensics lab we worked with originally used an image of three bottles in front of a lab tech on their home page, and it didn't mean anything to visitors. We chose a new image of a microscope, which was far more relevant to the company. It was a simple but effective change. In a crowded, noisy marketplace, you've got to find a way to cut through all the clutter and stand out. You can often do this through great images.

As you think through your website, you want to consider how it will connect to other marketing channels and efforts. For example, if you're doing an email campaign, one of the cardinal rules is to never send readers to your home page. Instead, you want to direct them to a landing page, which is a stand-alone web page created specifically for the purposes of a campaign. It's where a visitor "lands" when they click on a Google ad or link in your email.

If you're telling people about your authority in complex cases, you want to take them to a landing page with further information about complex cases, and then use a CTA that tells them what to do next. The CTA on the page might be "Download a white paper" or "Click here for a free consultation."

On any landing pages you build, you want to offer visitors something relevant that provides value. Video can be a great tool to increase conversion rate on your landing pages. According to Wordstream, using videos on landing pages will increase conversions by 86 percent.[3]

EMAIL

Email marketing is one of the most effective means of

---

3   "The Ultimate List of Marketing Statistics for 2018," Hubspot, accessed August 30, 2019, https://www.hubspot.com/marketing-statistics.

communication. It is just as great for launching new products as for customer engagement. This is why it's so crucial to build an email database. Through email, you can easily reach out to upsell, cross-sell, or engage new buyers.

In a single email, you can share photos, videos, and multiple messages or promotions. As mentioned, you can also use an email to drive readers to your website via links to specific and relevant landing pages. Thanks to marketing automation tools, you can even segment your database into different audiences based on the parameters you set, whether that's by industry, geography, or job title. You can then run email campaigns that target only a specific segment of your database.

If you're running an email campaign, remember to plan out a whole series of emails, not just one email. Also, be sure to keep the focus on adding value to the reader. You need to condition the market, not simply say, *Buy me now!* Make sure your prospects have the opportunity to get to know your company. Build a relationship of trust first before selling.

As you consider how to leverage email, make sure you are optimized for mobile technology. In 2018, 48 percent of emails were opened on a smartphone.[4]

---

4   Bettina Specht, "Email Client Market Share Trends," Litmus, July 13, 2018, https://litmus.com/blog/email-client-market-share-trends-first-half-of-2018.

SOCIAL MEDIA

To be successful in business, you need to reach your audience where they are. If your prospects are on a social media channel, that's where you need to be.

You can expand your reach by taking your weekly blog and amplifying it on social channels where your primary audience most often frequents. You should also have a plan for all of your employees to actively share approved content on your social media channels of choice. This is an easy and cost-effective way to drive traffic and stay in front of your clients and prospects.

To effectively engage your target audience on social media, it's important to understand how different platforms function. Here, we'll briefly review the most popular social networks as of 2019.[5] Keep in mind that the social media landscape is constantly changing, and new networks are bound to come on the scene.

FACEBOOK

Facebook sends more website referral traffic than any other social media network. It is oriented toward both entertainment and news, and it generally places a higher

---

5 "Most Popular Social Networks Worldwide as of January 2019," Statista, accessed August 30, 2019, https://www.statista.com/statistics/272014/global-social-networks-ranked-by-number-of-users/.

value on video content over other forms of content. Facebook touts 2.32 billion monthly active users as of December 31, 2018.

TWITTER

Twitter is as much a news platform as it is a social network. It allows you to source and share snippets of content and links. It is ideal for brands sharing blog posts or promoting website content. According to Statista, Twitter has 326 million monthly active users worldwide as of January 2019.

LINKEDIN

LinkedIn is a professional network where users can create profiles highlighting current and previous work experience, connect with colleagues, and build a professional network. It offers a built-in content publishing and distribution platform, and users can share industry articles and more. Video content is becoming more popular on this platform as well. If you're selling to CIOs and directors of IT, LinkedIn is a great option, particularly if you engage in CIO and IT groups. While you can't directly sell, you can gain credibility, authority, and trust by engaging and answering questions, and sharing relevant blog posts.

INSTAGRAM

Instagram is a photo-sharing app known for its square image format. It is built for mobile, although a desktop version is available for browsing. It is best suited for visual brands and is a great place to post static images and video (currently limited to sixty seconds).

PINTEREST

Pinterest is a highly visual platform that lends itself to strong imagery. The platform reaches a sizable audience, with more than 150 million "pinners." Users can browse Pinterest to see products, create wish lists, and even price and purchase from their mobile device with a few clicks. Those with a business account have additional features, such as analytics and the ability to advertise on the platform.

GOOGLE+

Google Plus is a social network that connects to other Google properties such as YouTube. It is oriented around communities that have particular interests.

YOUTUBE

YouTube is the biggest online video platform and features both individual user-generated content and corporate media content. With 1.9 billion users, it is a growing channel and one not to be ignored. We will discuss the importance of video in more detail below.

HASHTAGS

Finally, hashtags are words or phrases that are preceded by a hash mark (#). They are used on various social networks and make it easier for users to search and identify keywords and topics of interest. When you add a hashtag to your post, it will be indexed by the social network and becomes discoverable by other users via search.

To develop a hashtag that represents your brand, brainstorm ideas that best showcase your brand. The word or phrase needs to be short, and you want to make sure it is not already in use. Then use the hashtag on all social media and monitor how others use your hashtag so that you can respond accordingly. If you want to reach a certain audience, you can add an additional hashtag to your posts, such as #CEOs.

VIDEO

Many mid-market companies miss out on one communication channel that holds a lot of opportunity: video. Executives often have a wrong perception about the costs of video production; they might imagine, for example, that they will need to spend $10,000 to $15,000 to produce the perfect company video. They might think that making each video will require significant time and attention. Because of such thinking, many companies neglect video altogether.

The fact of the matter is that any company today can create videos in-house at very little cost. With an iPhone and a basic tripod, you can capture video with enough quality to get your messages across. Yes, there are always more expensive options, but those options would only make sense if video is a core communication method. For most companies, it is simply another communication channel to utilize.

At CenterBeam, we produced a new technical solution that was incredibly powerful for CIOs. The problem was that no one, except our CTO, could explain the solution fully. I could barely write about the new software integration because it was so complicated.

With a limited budget, we weren't sure how we could adequately communicate what we now had to offer. I suggested that we use my iPhone and a tiny tripod to film several snippets of our CTO being interviewed about the innovation we had developed.

Each video began with someone asking him a simple

question or prompt. They might say, "Tell us why this is so relevant for the mid-market CIO today." Then our CTO would share a brief explanation and the story behind the solution.

After we filmed him answering all the questions, we broke the video into parts, uploaded the snippets to YouTube, and embedded those onto our website. At the end of the day, we had spent nothing other than a small amount of time to share this critical information with the world.

When considering the use of video in your marketing, you should always keep your audience in mind. We live in a time in which visual learning is the norm. Millennials now expect to consume the majority of their information visually. Most millennials aren't going to read white papers the way previous generations did.

Why not serve rising generations the way they want to be served? With infographics and video, you can share information in a visual way and across social media channels. From those channels, you can direct viewers back to your main website.

You can use video to answer questions about a product, like we did at CenterBeam. You can also use video to support your sales process. If a sales rep can't answer an important question a prospect has, they can quickly pull up a video on a tablet or a phone.

Because video has become so widely used by businesses today, there are now ways to track its effectiveness. For example, basic video metrics can show you when most people stop watching the video.

If you keep your videos short, each with a clear message, you will find that many viewers watch until the end, and some viewers will also take an action—clicking a link to visit a landing page or reaching out to contact you.

YouTube is the second most trafficked site after Google, with over a billion active users. On mobile alone, You-Tube reaches more people in this US audience than any TV network. According to Forrester Research, one minute of video is worth 1.8 million words, because you're able to express a very complex message in just sixty seconds of video.[6]

Here are a few other interesting stats about video from sources such as Unbounce and Buffer:[7]

6   Kate Harrison, "Is Your Company Giving Video the Love It Deserves?" *Forbes*, March 31, 2016, https://www.forbes.com/sites/kateharrison/2016/03/31/is-your-company-giving-video-the-love-it-deserves/#6e08dfc464db.

7   "48 Video Marketing Statistics for 2018," Biteable, accessed August 31, 2019, https://biteable.com/blog/tips/video-marketing-statistics/.

- Viewers retain 95 percent of a message when they watch it on a video, compared to 10 percent when reading it in text.
- Companies that use video in their marketing have a 27 percent higher click-through rate and 34 percent higher conversion rate than those that don't.
- 59 percent of executives would rather watch a video than read text, which is a key point, particularly if you're targeting visual-learning millennials.

From a Hubspot 2018 research study, video was often cited as a tool that helps drive various areas of business performance, and the numbers back up those claims:[8]

- 97 percent of marketers say video has helped increase user understanding of their product or service.
- 76 percent say it helped them increase sales.
- 47 percent say it helped them reduce support queries.
- 76 percent say it helped them increase traffic.
- 80 percent of marketers say video has increased dwell time on their website.
- 95 percent of people have watched an explainer video to learn more about a product or service.
- 81 percent of people have been convinced to buy a product or service by watching a brand's video.

8   Adam Hayes, "The State of Video Marketing in 2019," Hubspot, January 24, 2018, https://blog. hubspot.com/marketing/state-of-video-marketing-new-data.

- 69 percent of people have been convinced to buy a piece of software or application by watching a video.
- 85 percent of people say they'd like to see more video from brands.

We have discussed how to set ourselves up for success with the right messages to the right targets on the right media. The next step is to select the most meaningful metrics to ensure we are driving the desired outcomes to the business. We need to focus on measuring the activities that matter most.

CHAPTER SEVEN

METRICS AND ITERATIONS

If you don't measure your marketing efforts, and act on the metrics you get, your sales team won't be effective. You'll waste a lot of time and money without getting results. This was illustrated perfectly when CenterBeam outsourced lead generation tracking to a great Atlanta-based agency called PointClear. We were targeting law firms in many verticals, and PointClear found that we achieved a 17 percent lead rate, which is pretty impressive.

Had we focused on only that data point, we would have focused all our efforts on reaching out to and calling law firms. Since our lead rate was that good, we could have assumed the win rate would be equally as impressive.

However, when we looked at data from further down the

funnel, we saw that we never closed with law firms. In the twelve-year history of the company, we never once won a single law firm.

When you're dealing with metrics, you have to look holistically at the full sales cycle. That way, you can know how to best move forward in both your marketing and sales efforts.

WHY MEASURE?

Some aspects of marketing, such as branding, are difficult to measure. Still, you should prioritize measurable marketing efforts and be selective about efforts that are less measurable. Remember that every dollar spent on an unmeasurable effort is a dollar that might have been validated. And the more you measure, the more you are able to effectively iterate as you go.

I recently worked with a company that thought they needed to be at every industry trade show. They would go and meet with customers and prospects, then move on to the next trade show. They spent a large portion of their marketing budget on this. When I asked what they were gaining from these shows, they couldn't tell me. They weren't measuring or tracking any of the results.

But if you do a trade show, you should have a strategy with

measurable goals so that you know whether you're getting a return on your investment. You need to establish how many leads, proposal opportunities, and wins you'll get from your investment.

UNDERSTAND THE TOP, MIDDLE, AND BOTTOM OF YOUR FUNNEL

At the top of your funnel, you want to create awareness. What are your awareness targets? How do you garner interest? In the middle of the funnel, you want to engage interested prospects. Here, you want to measure how many prospects actually turn into leads. Finally, at the bottom of the funnel, you want to track your sales and customer loyalty.

Here again is the example of a digital marketing funnel and elements you would want to track along the way for your reference.

DIGITAL MARKETING FUNNEL (ANALYTICS)

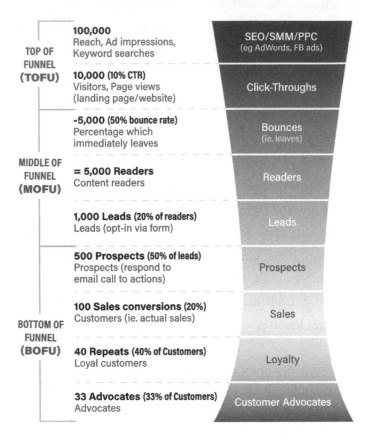

TOP OF FUNNEL (TOFU)	**100,000** Reach, Ad impressions, Keyword searches	SEO/SMM/PPC (eg AdWords, FB ads)
	10,000 (10% CTR) Visitors, Page views (landing page/website)	Click-Throughs
MIDDLE OF FUNNEL (MOFU)	**-5,000 (50% bounce rate)** Percentage which immediately leaves	Bounces (ie. leaves)
	= 5,000 Readers Content readers	Readers
	1,000 Leads (20% of readers) Leads (opt-in via form)	Leads
BOTTOM OF FUNNEL (BOFU)	**500 Prospects (50% of leads)** Prospects (respond to email call to actions)	Prospects
	100 Sales conversions (20%) Customers (ie. actual sales)	Sales
	40 Repeats (40% of Customers) Loyal customers	Loyalty
	33 Advocates (33% of Customers) Advocates	Customer Advocates

Every company needs to develop a digital marketing and sales funnel based on how their customers shop and use their products or services. Once you understand the big picture of your funnel, you can measure your success more accurately.

If you run an ad for awareness, you can see how many

impressions you get. If you write a new blog post, you can measure how many times people find you through a keyword search.

Once a prospect takes an initial action, you move to measuring the middle of the funnel. How quickly do people bounce off the site? How many people are reading your content? If someone reads your content and acts upon your call to action, you get a lead that turns into a prospect who wants to consider you. Then you can start the sales process.

Finally, if you measure how many times you win after you go through the sales process, you'll know your win rate. Then you can establish how to turn customers into loyal customers.

By analyzing your funnel and looking at your win rate, you can work out how to improve on it. If you don't get much organic traffic, for example, you'll need to put together a blog strategy. If your proposal win rate is less than 30 percent, then it is time for some insight on how to improve. A detailed funnel and metrics allow you to identify priority improvement areas.

TOOLS

There are many useful tools that help in measuring digital

marketing efforts. We'll review a few here, and you can find a more comprehensive list on the Cloudways blog.[9]

Websitegrader.com gives you an instant grade of your website's technical functions and provides recommendations for fixes and improvements. It takes only five minutes to gain valuable insights into your website performance.

You can also run a search engine optimization (SEO) competitive audit using a tool called Spyfu. This tool will show you the traffic of your top twenty-five competitors, and the traffic's behavior—how many pages they visit, how long they stay on the site, and the traffic sources. You can appropriate what's working for them and apply it to your own website. If one of your leading competitors is getting the majority of their traffic from Facebook, maybe you should focus your social media efforts on that channel. Very few companies take this step, so acting on it puts you ahead of the game.

Google Analytics is an excellent tool for metrics. It tells you how much traffic you're getting and where it's coming from. You can see how many new visitors you get to your website and how users behave on your site. You can gauge brand awareness by looking at direct traffic and engage-

---

9   Jamil Ali, "18 SEO Audit Tools for Effective Website Analysis," Cloudways, January 16, 2019, cloudways.com/blog/seo-audit-tools-list/.

ment by the number of returning visitors. For returning visitors, you want to track how often they move further down the funnel during their visit. Did they turn into a lead or get a quote?

When focusing on new prospects, look at your bounce rate. A high bounce rate means website visitors didn't get what they were looking for and bounced right off rather than clicking into multiple pages. To reduce your bounce rate, you'll need to do A/B testing to establish what works.

You can also use Google Analytics to see which words and phrases your visitors use most often and on which of your website pages they spent the most time, both of which can inform you about where to place your focus for further content development.

Google Analytics can also tell you how people are finding you. This is divided as follows:

- **Direct:** Direct visitors came directly to your website by typing in your URL right into their browser or clicking a link in an email. High direct traffic is a good indicator that your brand is strong.
- **Organic Search:** This traffic comes to your site via search engines such as Google and Bing. An organic visitor is someone who got to your website by clicking on a link from a search engine results page. High

organic traffic indicates the value of your content and SEO strategy.

- **Paid Search:** You can track Google AdWords campaigns, including conversions and cost per acquisition. High paid search traffic means that your Google AdWords strategy is working.
- **Referral:** This number shows visitors who clicked a link on another site to land on your website. High referral traffic means that you are being linked to from multiple other websites.
- **Social:** This shows what social media channels drive the majority of traffic to your site.
- **Email:** This shows the number of visitors who came to your website from an email campaign. This is a key metric to determine campaign effectiveness.

ITERATE

Are you making changes based on what you measure? You should be. You want to act on the data you gain from measuring. If you don't, it's pointless to measure in the first place.

You might have an amazing email database and a creative campaign, but if the email is not structured correctly or has too many links in it, you won't be getting the results you want or expect. In this case, you would need to understand what is getting in the way of results in order to make the necessary changes.

Analyzing your metrics on a weekly or monthly basis lets you see the big picture—are you progressing, regressing, or stagnating? Whatever tools you choose to use, establish your monthly goals or KPIs and use those to guide and support your strategy. Then go back to review and measure the data regularly.

It's also a good idea to keep a rolling twelve-month view so you can spot trends and visually see progress. You want to leave yourself plenty of time to tweak and proactively change course along the journey to make sure you meet your goals.

You'll want to take the same staggered approach to your overall marketing assessment, which we'll discuss in the next chapter.

CHAPTER EIGHT

MARKETING ASSESSMENT

Before you move ahead too quickly in sales efforts, you need to know how you're doing by running a marketing assessment. You want to see where your biggest issues are, where your biggest opportunities are, and where your immediate focus is required.

You can think of this assessment as a marketing report. The report will help you see the two or three areas where you need to place special attention. It will help you drive the most meaningful outcomes for the business.

Ideally, your marketing assessment should be conducted by an outside source, just as you would have an independent auditor review your finances. If you choose to do the assessment yourself, aim to be as objective as possible.

Here, I will review some of the key elements to include in your assessment.

ELEMENTS

Remember that all of your marketing efforts should always be guided by the voice of the customer. So you want to ask yourself: Are you collecting customer satisfaction data around buying and service? If not, how do you plan to start collecting this data?

Next up is customer insight. Have you completed a win-loss analysis at least once this year? As we've discussed, this lets you understand people's reasons for buying or deciding not to buy your products or services. You want to find out what steps those buyers took, what their buying process looked like.

Then comes the competitor landscape. Have you recently analyzed your main competitor's strengths and weaknesses? And have you developed a marketing strategy designed to beat out the competition?

Next up is SWOT. Have you completed a competitive SWOT analysis? And have you adequately activated against your strengths? Have you leveraged those strengths in your marketing plan? Remember that you activate against the analysis to find your best opportunities for growth. So how will you run SWOT analysis and respond to your findings moving forward?

Next, you want to ensure you have a current customer profile. Have you identified the most relevant characteristics of your perfect customers? If not, how do you plan to build out a buyer persona within the next quarter?

Here are a few more questions to round out your marketing assessment:

- Do you have a product roadmap that you can share with your customers?
- Have you done a competitive pricing review? When was the last time you took a price increase? Have you identified possible customer segments where a strategic price increase makes sense?
- Have you planned and budgeted for new customer acquisition?
- Is there a specific plan and budget for ensuring customer loyalty? How might you cross-sell other products/services to existing customers?
- Have you developed a product launch plan and process?
- Do you have an omni-channel lead generation process to identify, generate, and nurture qualified leads?
- Can you identify customers who will give you testimonials and be reference accounts?

- How will you leverage thought leadership and content strategy to create and deliver the information needed to influence prospects to buy? How will you distribute that information (blogs, e-books, videos, etc.)?
- Do you have an event strategy for generating awareness and leads at the top of the sales funnel?

As you answer the questions listed here, identify the biggest opportunities to grow the business and pick the most crucial two or three elements to focus on.

As you focus on the right marketing efforts, you will begin to see progress. However, marketing is only one piece to the puzzle. It's an important piece. It's where you need to begin. But now you need to take all you've learned and continue to pursue growth through executing effectively in your sales organization.

PART III

SALES EXECUTION FOR GROWTH

CHAPTER NINE

PROCESS AND METHODOLOGY

Even if you address your problems on the marketing side of the equation—if you eliminate random acts of marketing—you can still suffer from randomness in sales. If you want to have a predictable, profitable revenue plan, you need to apply discipline and consistency to your sales organization as well.

You can develop a *sales process* by analyzing your experience to date. A *focused methodology* will allow you to train your sales force effectively and create consistency in the entire team's approach to sales. Both process and methodology will ultimately allow you to align with marketing and support the "buy" cycle.

SALES PROCESS

First, let's consider how to develop a clear sales process in your organization. As mentioned, you develop a sales process by looking backward. You can begin by looking at and defining your ideal clients. What journey did they take that ultimately led them to a purchase? What didn't work for them along the way?

Review your last fifteen to twenty deals. As you look back, consider the specific steps you took with those fifteen or twenty deals in order to close the sale.

You might find, for example, that you did a demo with all twenty and that the demo typically came in step three. You might find that all of them had an inside sales touch-point to start the conversation, followed by a one-hour introductory call with the sales engineer or product specialist. These were the critical steps in the process that made the deals successful.

If you find that you never won a deal without doing a demo, that is critical data. The data tells you that doing a demonstration of the product or service with the prospect is essential. You should take that learning and include a demo step in your formal sales process and ensure sales reps never skip that essential step.

Along with reviewing deals, you want to review timelines. Let's say that you identify the average sales cycle is somewhere between 90 and 120 days—from the initial touchpoint to the signing of the order. Along that timeline, you will recognize the important people or stakeholders who were involved in the process. Did the prospect talk to the director of IT or the CIO at a particular point? When did that conversation occur? If the process started with a conversation with the CEO instead of the procurement office, was the cycle shortened?

By looking back and aligning around the facts, you can help get the marketing and sales organizations on the same page. As you are looking at deals, timelines, and people, you will inevitably recognize how prospects came to you in the first place, what questions they arrived with, or what information is most important to them. You can share that insight with marketing so they can help you have a more effective sales process and a fuller top of the sales funnel.

AN EXAMPLE SALES PROCESS

A typical sales process might include three to six emails or phone calls to get one discovery call. From the discovery call, you can qualify the opportunity (to see if they are the right person to speak to, in the right industry, and have an issue that is a priority). At this point, you might look to schedule a demo. After the demo, you would want to send two or three more follow-up emails to answer questions or provide deeper product information to the prospect. Finally, there would be a proposal and then a couple more follow-up emails before moving into negotiation mode.

Although you want to have a firm process to follow, you also need to be flexible. You need a plan B for when your sales process isn't possible. For example, at CenterBeam we were selling a managed IT service, and we knew we would get to the quickest close if someone could meet with the CFO. However, that wasn't always possible, so we sometimes set up meetings with the CIO instead.

Below is what our sales process looked like. We developed this process after looking back and identifying what worked well for us.

WELL-DEFINED SALES PROCESS

SUSPECT
- CFO meeting scheduled
- CRM opportunity created

PROSPECT · Initial business case scoped

QUALIFIED
- Cultural, technical, and financial fit defined
- Client environment analysis completed

PROPOSAL
- Business case presented
- Business case process/methodology

NEGOTIATION
- Validation meeting
- Monthly contract value
- Total satisfaction guarantee

WIN/LOSS · Contract in legal contract

Suspect/Prospect

Close

Order

Our sales process started out with a suspect who turned into a prospect, then became a qualified lead. This moved to a proposal that led to negotiation, then a win or loss.

We then defined all the outcomes that enabled us to identify where we were in the process. For example, if we scheduled a meeting with the CFO, we were still dealing with a suspect, whereas when we got an initial business case scope, they became a prospect. These clear definitions hold sales accountable for what stage in the funnel they are at and provide insight into sales velocity.

However clear you think your process is, it's crucial that you train your sales team to be utterly confident in it. Otherwise, you can't hold them accountable for it. Done correctly, the sales process will streamline your funnel, moving you from suspect to deal closure in the fastest possible time.

The process also helps with clarity when onboarding new salespeople. Even a great sales team has a staff turnover rate of up to 20 percent, so you're always hiring for sales roles. If you have a solid process in place that encapsulates all your best practices, you dramatically decrease the time it takes to train new assets and get them up to speed.

DEVELOPING THE METHODOLOGY

Sales methodology provides the framework for how different steps in your sales process are carried out. There are countless sales methodologies, and many are very similar or built around the same concept.

In *SPIN Selling*, released in 1980, Neil Rackham looked at the differences between highly successful salespeople and those who were underperforming. He showed that the successful sales reps asked higher-quality questions and built a methodology around this evidence.

Rackham showed that sales isn't just about aggressively pitching but also about asking insightful questions. He showed the importance of creating momentum by demonstrating that you are knowledgeable and understand the customer's needs. Buyers today are skeptical, and by the time they meet with a salesperson, they've done a lot of their own research. They may even know more about the category than the salesperson, so the initial step in a sales process is to gain trust. That should be built into every sales methodology.

TYPES

Challenger Selling, Consultative Selling, Solution Selling, and RAIN Selling are all popular methodologies. They are a few of the top-ten methodologies Charles Edge recommends on the Selling Power blog, a highly credible sales resource.[10]

Challenger Selling is about creating new ideas and challenging old assumptions. Following this methodology, you have to present new ideas and information that demonstrates a high degree of interest in the client, creates trust, and differentiates you from other salespeople they may encounter.

Consultative Selling is based on the idea that the salesperson should become a prospect's trusted advisor.

Solution Selling is about focusing on a prospect's pain points so you can offer a solution rather than a product.

RAIN Selling has three elements: connect, collaborate, convince. First, you connect with customers and understand their needs in order to build a relationship with them and craft compelling solutions. Once you build a meaningful connection, then you need to collaborate with them. Rather than push your ideas onto the client, you listen and respond by bringing value to the situation. Finally, you convince them that your solution is the one that'll provide the results they're looking for.

---

10   Charles Edge, "The Top 10 Sales Methodologies You Should Consider for Your Business," July 27, 2016, https://blog.sellingpower.com/gg/2016/07/the-top-10-sales-methodologies-you-should-consider-for-your-business.html.

Whether you create your own or choose one of these, you need to include the foundational elements of insightful questions and building momentum through trust.

One of the questions the Chief Outsiders team asks is, "Where do you think Chief Outsiders can offer the most value to you?" A question like this comes after you've had a long dialogue with the client about their business and about yours, and you ask this question to find out what's resonating with them. You can then take your direction from the client's answer.

Even though you want to ask good questions, prospects should never feel like they are being interrogated. Instead, structure and sequence your questions in a logical and coherent way that makes the customer feel like they're engaged in a customer-centric dialogue. By listening and fostering trust, you can put forward your company's most appropriate offering.

RECRUITING SALESPEOPLE

Just as you have a sales process and method of selling, you likewise need a method to ensure you get the best ROI possible from the talent you hire. The talent will, after all, be the ones implementing your sales process and methodology.

In enterprise environments, a salesperson might not get

an order for eight to twelve months. That means you carry an expensive FTE who might not deliver results for up to a year. Because of this reality, you don't need the added risk of having someone who can't deliver when it comes time.

One of my bosses at Xerox had a famous saying: "Inspect what you expect." That's the mantra to follow when hiring salespeople. Some salespeople are nothing more than glorified administrative assistants who were heavily guided by executive involvement. They don't have the insight or business acumen to perform successfully on their own.

Define the skills you need the person to have, and then test for them. If the person tells you they developed business cases, get on GoToMeeting or Zoom with them and have them present to you the last one they won.

I have seen salespeople with incredible résumés perform poorly when tested. Why? Well, let's say you're a salesperson at Xerox and want to do an enterprise sale with a large bank. In that case, you might work on that account for one or two years, with a lot of executive involvement. Executives shepherd the proposal and establish close executive relationships with those who really make a difference in winning the order. On your résumé, you can legitimately write that you closed a billion dollars of software sales with a large bank.

If you're considering this person as a potential hire, however, you should never rely solely on the information contained in their résumé or from their references. You need to know what you can actually expect. Rather than rely solely on a headhunter, invest time to truly test applicants. If you are hiring salespeople who will need to write proposals, give them a test to write a proposal. If you're hiring someone who's going to do presentations, have them do a presentation for you.

Also determine role-plays you will use for each candidate so you can see the ability the person has to think on their feet. My best practice is to give the person a sales scenario. I create a fictional case study with an irate customer. I say, "You walk into the office and find out about this irate customer. Their deliveries were late." I ask them to role-play with me. I give them fifteen minutes to think about what to do, and then I see how they perform. It's often astonishing how poorly well-seasoned sales professionals perform under pressure. The experience is truly eye-opening.

After giving these initial test cases, I recommend giving a test sales call. You can again create a fictional situation and tell them the rules. You can explain they are calling a certain person and explain what they understand about the prospect so far. Make it a scenario that they might face at the job level.

Don't forget to also test for interpersonal skills. B2B selling is not a lone-wolf game; it's a team sport. Active listening and empathy are crucial to work in the team and to work with prospects. You can get a clear impression of who someone is from each call and test. See how well they listen. What is their questioning technique? Do they ask open-ended or close-ended questions? Are there awkward pauses? Are they personable? If someone has good interpersonal skills, they are much more likely to perform well in the role.

You can also rely on tests such as the one from Objective Management Group (OMG), which is a sales assessment company that offers several sales-specific assessments for sales reps, managers, and directors/VPs. Other tests include Predictive Index, The DISC Profile, and StrengthsFinder. Each of these will provide further insight into your sales candidates.

Now that you have a plan in place for your sales process and methodology and know how to build your sales team, it's time to consider tools that can enable you to sell more efficiently and effectively.

CHAPTER TEN

SALES ENABLEMENT

As you consider how to best approach sales, it's important to understand how your customers are buying today. Yes, you might agree that people do research and shop online, but have you stepped back and asked, "What does this imply for my sales team and my business?" The reality is that prospects are self-educating online before they ever engage with you, so your prospects are coming to you more knowledgeable than ever before.

Prospects research before they decide whom to meet or not meet. This is why marketing had to come first in our discussion. This is where the entire sales process begins. However, when a prospect does end up talking to your sales team, the team needs to be equipped with the right tools to close the order.

THIRD-LEVEL QUESTIONS

Today, your sales team needs to be equipped to answer third-level questions.

I met a CEO who described to me the challenge he faced trying to keep his salespeople trained with his deeply technical home windows product. He told me that the customers already knew more than his sales reps before they ever engaged. He also knew that if he could respond to prospects better than his competitors did—who faced the same issue—he would have a significant competitive advantage.

He described to me the situation. His customers would go online, do their research, and choose two companies to further consider. By the time they met with the sales team, they didn't need a big presentation. They were concerned with the intricate technical details of the windows. They asked what I call third-level questions such as, "How does this feature work? What's the difference between these two options?"

I worked with this CEO to create a helpful solution for this sales team: a series of short videos. Each video contained a quick interview with subject-matter experts answering key questions. When a prospect asked a third-level question, the salesperson could say, "Let me show you this thirty-second or sixty-second video to answer that question." In turn, the prospects got the right information from the person best positioned to give it.

SALES ENABLEMENT TOOLS

You might discover that you need other sales enablement tools to respond to your specific prospect needs.

At CenterBeam, we found that our prospects wanted to understand our pricing. Industry practice was to never reveal price until you understood the prospect's costs. So we built a calculator that guided our prospects through the pricing so they could see their costs, along with all the costs our services offset. This collaborative approach was totally transparent, so it built trust.

Some companies develop even more complex calculators that spit out value propositions for the customer based on their answers to a series of questions. Other sales enablement tools online include a proposal generator, demos, free trials, and white papers.

PATH TO CLOSURE

Sales enablement is all about giving your salespeople what they need, when they need it. I developed a method called path to closure, which is a simple but effective method your salespeople can use to understand what needs to happen from a customer point of view to close the deal.

I developed this method when I was at Xerox selling big-ticket items. With each new prospect, I would say, "I see that you're interested in this piece of equipment or these services. Could you walk me through your timeline? What are the steps to make this happen? And when do you envision this being up and running?" Essentially, I was asking them to tell me what steps it would take to close out the transaction.

You always want to start with the "go live" date and then work backward on the key milestones in order to achieve that go-live date. In subsequent sales meetings, make sure you pull up the timeline to make sure you are on track and address any new developments. The key to success is making this a collaborate, joint effort with your customer. Below is an example of what the path to closure timeline might look like.

PATH TO CLOSURE

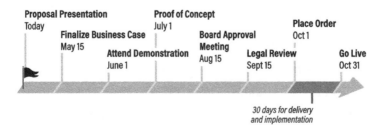

Proposal Presentation
Today

Finalize Business Case
May 15

Attend Demonstration
June 1

Proof of Concept
July 1

Board Approval
Meeting
Aug 15

Legal Review
Sept 15

Place Order
Oct 1

Go Live
Oct 31

30 days for delivery
and implementation

Every path to closure is different, because every prospect will have a different set of steps in their process. But if you can get this kind of information from your prospects, you can better serve them through the buying process and better forecast when the sale will close.

Imagine that you go to a networking event and meet a prospect who is super-keen on your product. They ask you all the relevant questions and express so much enthusiasm that you think you've got a really hot lead. You could say, "We'd love to work with you. What's your timeline? When do you want this to go live?" If they respond and tell you they don't need it until a few years out, they are no longer such a hot lead. However, they might say that they need the product live in a year.

In this case, you might respond, "Well, our process takes seven months, so why don't you walk me through your milestones? Who makes the final decision? Who releases the budget and when? On a scale of 1 to 10, how committed is the organization to making this change?" The more specifics they provide in their answers, the more you know where to spend your time and resources.

NO TOOLS REPLACE THE CUSTOMER PERSPECTIVE

When I landed a position as sales manager at Xerox, it

was a milestone job because there were very few female sales managers at that time. Naturally, I was driven to prove I could succeed. I clearly remember one of the first meetings I had with a prospect, the CEO of a financial services company in Toronto.

My sales rep and I did our research beforehand and put together some calculations. When we met with the CEO, we told him right away that we could save him $80,000 per year by upgrading his photocopier and trading out his lease. He kindly but pointedly said, "Karen, I don't get out of bed for less than $150,000 per deal, so saving $80,000 is just not interesting to me. The amount of time I'd have to invest to read and prioritize your contract doesn't make it worth the savings."

This experience taught me an important lesson. No matter how well I thought I was equipped, each sales path needed to be based on what was important to the customer. I thought saving $80,000 a year was a big deal; he didn't. It was through this experience that I discovered the best sales enablement tool: finding the most important question.

DRIVE DOWN TO THE MOST IMPORTANT QUESTION

When you're having an initial conversation with a

decision-maker, my number-one rule is that it's better to be interested than interesting. You have to show this person that you're genuinely interested in understanding their priorities and finding the right solutions for their problems. Because all pain is not created equal, it is not enough to simply find the pain; you must also determine the person's priorities. Ultimately, business resources (time and money) are allocated to solutions that support those priorities.

In sales, you need to be well informed about your leads. A cardinal rule is to never ask a client a question that could have been answered with online research. Before you go into a meeting or call, you should do your research. There are tools available that scan public records and put together a brief for you, identifying a company's corporate priorities.

At the same time, you also need to be open to discovery. Don't just go and pitch. Good business development starts with an authentic conversation to uncover priority issues and buying criteria. Stop and listen to your prospect. Get to know them and the issues they need solutions for.

You might assume a reduced turnaround time is your key selling point, but some of your prospects might be more interested in ongoing communication and a shorter deployment time frame. Because each prospect is different, you need to first listen so you can better direct your sales effort to focus on being relevant to each buyer.

When a prospect already understands your offerings, it is important to question one level deeper. You might say something like, "Okay, you've already done your homework and you understand the product and the competitive landscape. Where do you think that we could offer the biggest value for you?" This question gets the buyer to tell you what they value and shows you how they want to be sold to.

The prospect might say, "I think the biggest value is that I could get access to instantaneous engineering support in my local area without having to put someone on a plane." Take the opportunity to go deeper and ask, "Why is that so important to you?" Once you have identified that engineering resource proximity is most important to them and why, then you can make sure to emphasize that point in your proposal and in your follow-up conversations.

I have seen how important listening is from both a sales side and the customer side. At one point, I had a direct sales team that wasn't successfully closing deals, so I looked for consultants to provide solutions. One consultant came in and told me I should consider a channel strategy. The problem was that this strategy wasn't relevant to me. It might have led to more potential deals, but that wasn't my problem. My problem was with closing. If an internal sales team couldn't close an order, it was even less likely that someone in a channel organization could. We needed help accelerating our own win rate before we looked to broader distribution.

In short, this consultant offered a factory-out product, not a customer-in solution. He focused on what he could do, not what I needed. Had he asked me about my biggest challenge and priority, he could have easily positioned himself to get my business.

The lesson here is clear: always use the tools at your disposal, but keep the focus on the prospect. Do your up-front research. Understand the priorities and make sure the issue you are solving for is attached to a corporate priority. Be ready to listen and find the questions that matter most in each scenario.

CHAPTER ELEVEN

TARGETING LARGE ACCOUNTS

With large businesses today, many more stakeholders are involved in a sale. Whereas you could once talk to a CFO for procurement and an operations person for the purchase, you now need to engage the VP of the division, the director of the division, and more. A 2014 study from IDG Enterprise found that there are typically seventeen people influencing an enterprise purchase, compared to just ten in 2011.[11] The number of stakeholders involved in a sale has only continued to grow, making enterprise selling significantly more challenging.

Not only do you need to know how to effectively engage the right people at these companies, but you also need

---

11   IDG, "Role & Influence of the Technology Decision-Maker 2014," February 25, 2015, https://www.idg.com/tools-for-marketers/role-influence-of-the-technology-decision-maker-2014/.

to be prepared with the right information that is relevant to them. Your goal is to reach as many stakeholders as possible and keep all of them engaged.

WHO AND HOW

How do you reach large accounts? What message do you need to deliver to all relevant stakeholders to pique their interest? If you skip over an important stakeholder, that one person can derail the deal you've spent a year chasing.

Whenever possible, match up relevant connections between the two companies. If your company has an executive who knows an executive in the account's company, it makes sense to get those two together. That gives you a foundation of trust to work from. If you don't find any connections, take time to map out who the decision-makers are and come up with a strategy to reach them. You could first reach out digitally or plan to meet at a networking event or trade show.

The graphic below outlines how to match your message to the level of person you are dealing with in an enterprise sales cycle. If you are talking to the CEO or a C-level executive, they are interested in the outcomes you can deliver for their organizations and are best approached at a strategic level with a longer time horizon. They are looking for ways to move their organizations forward. Always remember they can access discretionary funds.

Those buyers in the middle of the organization's structure and the first- and second-level managers/directors often manage multiple budgets and can move funds from one budget center to another. Because they manage work processes, they appreciate a consultative approach.

When dealing with frontline individual contributors, they are operationally focused and have a tactical orientation. They have a short time horizon for problem-solving.

Looking at this chart, you can see exactly why you would never talk to a CEO about product function and features; if you do, you'll be quickly flushed down the organization with a comment like, "Bill Smith in procurement takes care of those things."

MESSAGE HAS TO MATCH LEVEL

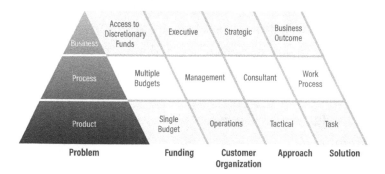

Working with large accounts always requires multiple steps. You need to establish the entire communication series for each persona in the stakeholder group. Your first line of communication could be something simple like, "I'd like to meet to discuss what our company has been doing to help others in your industry fill particular needs and to understand how your business has been addressing those needs." If that communication is successful, you then need to keep the momentum by continuing the dialogue.

If you do get a chance to speak with the CFO, it's not time to bamboozle him or her with technical specifications. You want to instead speak in terms of ROI. What are their priorities? Find a way to respond directly to those.

Follow that course with each stakeholder. Find their priorities and respond. When I sold to a public company at Xerox, I first read their SEC (Securities and Exchange Commission) filing and looked at how the executives were paid. I found out that they had been measured, in part, by customer satisfaction, so I found a way to show them how our product could help them achieve a better score on that metric. To speak about ROI is one thing, but if you can talk to each stakeholder about their individual bank balances, you'll have even more of their attention.

BUILDING TRUST

An account-based sales and marketing approach involves segmenting the different groups in a company and targeting each according to their interests. The technology you use is secondary. The key here is to gain access to the right people with a relevant message and to build the trust of all stakeholders. For example, you can utilize technical sales support personnel to speak with engineering stakeholders about relevant industry topics.

Account-based sales is effective when pursuing big accounts because it requires the sales team to listen and learn about the prospect through ongoing discovery and communication. It makes each interaction with the lead highly relevant. A mass email blast will not work here. You need to send and communicate personalized messages in each digital outreach.

By personalizing your communication with large accounts, you will sell more and have faster close rates. In an article titled "The New Sales Imperative" in the *Harvard Business Review*, the authors wrote, "Suppliers that make buying easy are 62% likelier than other suppliers to win a high-quality sale (one in which the customer buys a premium offering). In fact, purchase ease is by far the biggest driver of deal quality we've found across three large studies."[12]

---

12 Nicholas Toman, Brent Adamson, and Cristina Gomez, "The New Sales Imperative," *Harvard Business Review*, March–April 2017, https://hbr.org/2017/03/the-new-sales-imperative.

Even though you want to increase your rate to close, you always need to prepare for much more than initial conversation when you're working with large accounts. Develop deep, meaningful relationships with them. Your efforts will pay off for years to come.

CHAPTER TWELVE

DELIVERING PROPOSALS

———

At EarthLink, we had a large inside sales organization, but we had an abnormally low win rate on our proposals. We did a root cause analysis to find out why and quickly learned that we were too quick to send them out. We'd do a discovery call, and the lead would agree to look at a proposal. Our sales rep would email one over right away, then chase the lead for feedback—often to no avail.

We slowed down our process and collaborated closely with prospects to truly understand their buying criteria and the priority problem that they needed to solve. We asked if they fully understood what we meant by each feature, benefit, and delivery promise. By making these changes, our win rate on proposals shot up considerably.

There is a right way and a wrong way to send proposals.

Here, I want to walk through the most critical elements of getting proposals right.

DON'T BE IN A HURRY

Many salespeople are too quick to send out proposals. They slap something together and hurry it out the door without any real collaboration with the prospect. Yes, they manage to meet a goal of sending out a lot of proposals, but if they aren't quality proposals, they're doing the company a disservice.

Simply emailing a generic proposal and then chasing the lead isn't effective. Unless you have a marketing automation solution in place, you won't even know if the recipient opens your email.

Putting a proposal together costs time and resources, so you want to deliver the one that's likely to generate a sale. Before you ever send a proposal, you should first talk to your prospect about what they want to see in it. Say, "Based on our previous interactions, here's what we understand your biggest problems and issues to be, and here's where we believe we can offer the most value." Again, keep in mind that all pain is not equal. You want to find the pain that is attached to a corporate priority. When you talk to a prospect, it's not time to talk about how great you are. It's time to find their pain and address it.

Their answer will show you what they're looking for and will allow you to answer any misunderstandings of what you can offer. With proposals, we're again working from the premise that good selling requires active listening and momentum built through trust.

USE YOUR PROPOSAL TO QUALIFY

Many salespeople make the mistake of qualifying a lead, sending them a proposal by email, then chasing them by phone and email. But this tactic misses out on a crucial step. It's far more effective to say, "It would be presumptuous of me to think that in just a couple of meetings I know everything I need to about your business. Therefore, I'd like to prepare a proposal draft for you, then we can meet and review it together, make any changes we agree on, and then you'll have a solid proposal we can move forward with."

Set up the draft review meeting in Zoom or some other virtual conference room where you can share the document, connect with a client, and collaborate on it live. The level of complexity of your service will determine how much time you need to spend with the prospect, but by reviewing it together, you gain important insights. On this call, you can talk about timeline and path to closure to get everybody on the same page.

If the prospect doesn't want to give you an hour of their

time to collaborate, then they aren't really interested, so save your resources and don't bother creating a proposal.

With Chief Outsiders, I always present a draft proposal first. I'll say to the prospect, "This is the terminology we use. Are you familiar with this, or would you like me to clarify?" Frequently, they'll ask me to clarify and provide examples. I don't mind this at all. I want them to be comfortable and fully understand the entire proposal and what they would get out of an engagement with us. By sending a draft, I can also catch any changes that have come up in a client's needs since the discovery call.

If you get a proposal wrong, it can destroy all the time, effort, and resources you've poured into nurturing the lead. If you get it right, you can use it to qualify and close quality leads.

CHAPTER THIRTEEN

OBJECTION HANDLING

———

I've seen many business opportunities frittered away simply because someone in sales or technical sales engineering didn't know how to handle a prospect's objections.

Do those in your organization know how to handle the top-ten objections they hear from prospects? They must if you want to improve sales productivity and win rate. Train your sales team in this area, and share the knowledge more broadly with anyone in your organization who may come into contact with customers.

At CenterBeam, we started with only one significant client, a publication. We quickly gained more clients, but our sales team still encountered difficult situations. For example, prospects would say, "Tell me who else you have in the manufacturing space." The sales team didn't know what to say except to admit that we didn't have anybody in that space and that they'd be our first. Needless to say, their answer was uninspiring for a prospective buyer. Even though our service was horizontal in nature, clients still felt the solution would be less risky if we were serving others in their same industry.

So we had to teach our sales team how to deal with this. In this instance, we trained them to say to the client, "Even if I gave you another manufacturing company we were serving as reference, their IT processes would be handled totally differently than yours. Would you agree?" They'd usually give their agreement, so the salesperson could say, "Well, let me tell you about our ability to be flexible to your unique process." The salesperson could then describe the work we had done with different companies, large and small, and the way we adapted to each of them, showcasing our flexibility and how that could be translated to the manufacturing industry and this particular company.

FINDING OBJECTIONS

You need to know the top objections you will face and know how you will respond. This tactic works exceptionally well, unless you are selling to businesses that are highly regulated. For example, if you're targeting an industry that requires HIPAA compliance, you need to be able to address that specific requirement.

There are a couple of options for finding your top-ten objections. You can start with a win-loss analysis to find out why you didn't win certain accounts. Maybe the client thought you were too expensive, or maybe you didn't clearly convey cost of ownership or your value proposition. You can also ask your sales force. They'll tell you the key objections they hear from prospects on a regular basis, but remember that this sometimes isn't enough. Sometimes you need to hire an outside resource for lost customers to really open up.

No matter your tactic for finding objections, it's important to not turn off to them. Objections may be frustrating, but they aren't necessarily the customer's way of saying no.

When a prospect is going through the buying process, they constantly ask questions such as, "Am I going to get the benefit I need?" or "Is it worth the risk I'm going to take to make the change?" You might hear some of their concerns as objections. For example, they might say, "We don't understand the ongoing service costs." In this case, they are simply missing information, and you can easily reconcile that.

In many cases, the prospect simply needs to clarify something, but they phrase it as an objection. They might say, "I'm concerned that your customer service team is too small to respond immediately to our needs." This statement could be borne out of the misguided assumption that your service desk consists of one person rather than a whole team. Again, this is easy to correct.

In other cases, the objection is a smokescreen. A prospect will give you a vague response like, "You're too expensive," or "We heard you weren't reliable." These statements might not be true, but they think it's an easy way to get rid of you rather than telling you their real issues. For this reason, you want to always get to the heart of their objection.

GETTING TO THE HEART OF IT

To not have flat-footed salespeople without a response, I teach them objection handling with three key points—Stop. Listen. Clarify.

Step one—you've got to hear them out completely. Don't interrupt. This step is all about active listening.

Step two—clarify the objection. As mentioned, a prospect's initial "objection" isn't actually their concern, so it's your job to try to understand what caused them to object and what the real issue is. Listen to hear, not to speak. Be empathetic. Show the prospect that you've heard them and understand how they feel. You could say, "Some of my best clients felt the same way, so I completely understand. I recognize this is a big decision for you, and you want to make sure it's the right one." Here, you don't want to make the mistake of jumping right to the solution. Restating the objection demonstrates empathy and shows the client that you listened and that you understand.

Once you've restated and clarified, you can tell the prospect that you may have skipped a few relevant details, and request their consent to explain. This makes the customer feel like they're in control. In most cases, they will give you permission to sell to them more directly.

Now it's your chance to answer their objection. If they say their objection is that it's too expensive, you could respond with, "I understand how you feel. It's hard to justify cost if you can't see the value." In this case, it's important to refer back to their answer to, "Where is it you see the biggest value?" Remind them of their answer so they can think of value based on their own words.

If they don't see the value themselves, you need to walk them through it. Isolate the objective by saying, "Okay, let's just set price aside for now. If everything were equal, would you be comfortable choosing our company?" Or "If our services fit within your budget, is this the solution you feel is really right for your company?" You start to dig a little deeper and get a more insightful answer.

Often, this is when the prospect will tell you what their real concern is. They might share that they are actually concerned by your security model or the way you deliver your service. This is your chance to ask them to expand on that concern and to listen. Repeat their concern back to them again to show you're still hearing them. After clarifying their issue, provide them with some technical information, some data, a white paper, or any other piece of sales collateral that clearly responds to their concern. In this way, you can allay their concerns and move the conversation forward.

Most salespeople make the mistake of answering an objection, then plowing on, still talking. This is called talking past the close. The danger here is that you will introduce new objections. Instead, you should stick to your scripted response. Answer their objection and come to closure on it. Ask them, "Does that answer your concern?" Once they confirm, you have closure and you can stop talking. You can then ask the prospect if they are ready to proceed.

Prospects will often say they need to show your offerings to their boss or business partner. In these cases, you still have the opportunity to isolate the objection and move forward. In this instance, you could say, "Okay, that makes perfect sense. Now let me ask you—if, after you show it to your CEO and he said, 'Okay, go ahead'—is this something you'd want to move forward with?"

Again, this helps get beyond their superficial response and starts to get at the real issue. If the prospect tells you they do want to move forward if they get approval, you have the opportunity to collaborate and turn the prospect into your ally by saying, "Great, I take it you'll recommend us to the CEO, then? What can we do to make sure he agrees with us?"

I always recommend writing out your top-ten objections and the appropriate responses. Why? Because it's difficult to think on your feet unless you've been selling a product for years, particularly in the digital era, where products and services are often complex. You want to equip your sales force with all the help they can get to overcome these objections and drive forward opportunities that would otherwise be lost.

USE OBJECTIONS TO YOUR ADVANTAGE

Listing your top-ten objections has another benefit, too—it lets you identify opportunities to answer or overcome objections before a prospect even reaches the sales team.

For example, if you sell aluminum garden tools, your potential customers might want to know why your aluminum ones are better than iron or stainless-steel ones. In this case, you could have your top engineer create a blog post around that specific topic and share it widely on social media.

If you're answering the questions people already have when they're researching and considering purchasing your product, Google will reward you with higher search engine rankings. So take your top-ten objections and assign them to the relevant subject-matter experts. Have them write first drafts, and then have a copy editor go over them to ensure they are flawless and optimized for SEO.

These articles will also be helpful for your sales force and customer service teams. Now they have detailed information ready to go when a client raises one of the objections. So not only are you increasing organic traffic and authority in your field, but you are also making your sales process more efficient and effective.

When prospects already have most of their questions answered when they come to sales, and then the sales rep addresses any remaining concerns, they will enter the post-sale relationship with a higher degree of trust. They fully understand your company and your offerings.

Remember, objections are not rejections; they're simply questions that need to be answered. Even if a prospect has multiple objections, you can still close the sale if you

don't make the objection personal but instead look at it
through the customer's eyes.

CHAPTER FOURTEEN

EXECUTIVE PROGRAM WITH TOP ACCOUNTS

———

While I was general manager of sales operation at Xerox in Toronto, one of our accounts, Mail Boxes Etc., was at risk. We were being outsold by our biggest competitor and our yearly revenue from that account was in significant decline.

At Xerox, as well as almost all *Fortune* 1,000 companies, it's standard for each senior executive to have at least one focus account. Because sales has such a high turnover, it's dangerous to leave the most important accounts to sales reps and first-line managers. It is the executive's responsibility to meet with their assigned client quarterly and develop strategic relationships with multiple people within the organization.

In the case of Mail Boxes Etc., I met Michael Martino, their CEO in early 1993. The truth was that Xerox had taken their eye off the ball, and this significant account was declining in a major way. We discussed over a long lunch Michael's key concerns, and I made a commitment to fix the issues. I told him, "Here's my goal: I want to be your number-one strategic partner for all your system and equipment needs, and I will work hard to turn this situation around. Let's talk about how we can build this plan together. I need you to give me a chance. The first time I falter, all bets are off." Because I was involved in such a personal way, he agreed.

It would have been difficult for a sales rep to make the time and resource investment that I was able to make. A sales rep's time horizon can be very short and their behavior opportunistic. As an executive, I was able to take a longer-term view of what was needed to turn the situation around, and I had access to senior resources. I was Michael's champion inside Xerox. I met monthly with our service managers and the VP of service operations and enlisted their support to be more in tune and responsive to the client's needs. In turn, I regularly reviewed our progress and continuous improvement with the client, further building the personal relationship.

Ultimately, we turned this major but declining account around in less than eight months and turned it into one of our fastest-growing accounts. We then further capitalized on this by leveraging this solid relationship with the client's parent company in the United States. This example shows how important the executive program with a top account can be.

ASSIGNING EXECUTIVES

The general rule of thumb is that 20 percent of your clients drive 80 percent of your revenue, yet most businesses treat all of their customers equally. Your time and resources are limited, so you have to decide which clients to focus most of your resources on.

Identify the largest clients in terms of revenue—those whose departure would have the biggest negative impact on your business. Of those, pinpoint the client who is the biggest risk, and assign the best qualified executive to this account. Then make sure every other member of the executive team has at least one account.

You can decide the right fit based on which connections make sense. For example, if one of your top accounts has a lot of administration issues, it makes sense to give that one to your VP of account administration. You can also match executives with accounts geographically. If you have an executive in San Francisco and he has small children, he most likely doesn't want to travel to New York regularly, so give him an account closer to home.

GAINING INSIGHT AND RESPONDING

Fortune 1,000 companies assign executives to their top accounts for a reason. First, it builds the relationship between the two companies. Second, it allows them more direct access to other relevant people in the company.

At CenterBeam, the CEO and I had worked together at Xerox Canada. We were both familiar with the Focus Executive program, and we decided to implement it at CenterBeam. Each of our executives was assigned an account to ensure we were developing broader and deeper relationships with top accounts.

This program will also help you validate what issues are most important. When our CFO went to meet with the focus account he'd been assigned, he came back and made it abundantly clear that our billing system needed to be fixed immediately. The sales team had already been complaining about this, so we knew now that we had to place focus on this area. When you have a direct channel of communication between the client and an executive, you ensure customers are heard by those who can bring about real change. In this case, the billing system was rapidly fixed to relieve customer aggravation.

This program will also allow you to further build your competitive advantage. When our CEO met with his focus account, his client asked him to develop specific reporting to give him deeper visibility and results by geography. By responding to this request for a new reporting feature, we essentially built a competitive advantage into our IT service.

REDUCING CHURN

It's just as important to have a strategy to retain your customers as it is to get new ones, especially when it comes to your top accounts. If you're an annuity business, you need to pay even more attention to churn. Research indicates that it's up to six times more expensive to acquire a new customer than to keep an existing one.[13] And if you're not convinced that retaining customers is so valuable, consider research done by Frederick Reichheld of Bain & Company (the inventor of the Net Promoter Score) that shows that increasing customer retention rates by 5 percent increases profits by 25 to 95 percent.[14]

Some businesses, particularly in the managed services sector, have a churn rate of up to 50 percent. At Center-

---

13   Tricia Morris, "It Is 6 Times More Expensive to Win a New Customer Than to Retain an Existing One," Business2Community, March 20, 2016, https://www.business2community.com/strategy/6-times-expensive-win-new-customer-retain-existing-one-01483871.

14   Fred Reichheld, "Prescription for Cutting Costs," Bain, accessed August 31, 2019, http://www2.bain.com/Images/BB_Prescription_cutting_costs.pdf.

Beam, we had virtually no churn. The only time we lost a customer was when they were sold to a larger entity or ceased business operations. Our churn was so low largely because of our Focus Executive program and the deep trust relationships we built with our clients.

One of my focus accounts was the Colorado University Foundation. Their CFO called me one Saturday morning because he had a serious issue. I responded right away, as he knew I would, because we'd built a trusting relationship over the eight years we'd worked together. Because of that deep connection and executive access, it would've been difficult for him to cancel our arrangement and take his business elsewhere without engaging me first to remedy the situation.

By building deep and wide relationships, you also mitigate risk related to changes in personnel. You don't have to rely on a single sales rep or on one contact in the customer organization. Moreover, these relationships provide better account coverage to find more opportunity.

CONTINUING THE CONVERSATION

Although the executive is the main point of contact for each focus account, he or she may not be the best person to resolve every issue. Executives need to act as conductors, bringing in different resources as necessary.

For example, working with the University of Colorado Foundation, I was the point person, but I wasn't the most technical on our team. So, as needed, I'd bring in our CTO and ask him to provide a technical update to the client. Or I'd bring in my VP of call center operations to conduct an operations review on our help-desk services.

Everybody at CenterBeam also knew I was the point person for this account, so if the client ever had a server go down, I'd be informed and could call the CEO right away, before he knew there was a problem, and let him know that we were on it and that the problem would be fixed in the next ninety minutes. This kind of ongoing relationship obviously builds trust and loyalty and, just as importantly, grows revenue and protects against churn.

Once again, it's important to remember that sales goes beyond pitching. It involves listening and building high-trust relationships.

If you employ the executive program in your business, your top clients will try hard to give you all of their business. They will likely feel so connected to you that they will refer you to other businesses as well. The deep connections you build will allow you to win over the long haul.

CHAPTER FIFTEEN

SALES ASSESSMENT

Just as you can benefit from a marketing assessment, you can benefit from doing a sales assessment. You can self-assess by asking yourself a few key questions.

First, do you have a sales process and methodology that is deployed consistently across the organization? Have you implemented a sales methodology tailored to your business's sales cycle?

Next, how do you measure your results in sales? Do you have weekly, monthly, and quarterly reporting by sales rep, by sales team, by geography? Do you have a monthly sales forecast, and are you satisfied with its accuracy? Do you have weekly sales meetings to review the pipeline and ensure there are enough opportunities to adequately make the revenue targets?

If you have high turnover on your sales team, ask what you can do to lower that, since it costs the company each time you need to hire someone new. A highly transactional sales force reacts well to being rewarded weekly. However, if you have longer sales cycles of twelve months or more, it makes more sense to recognize achievements quarterly or annually.

Also, ensure you're using the right metrics to measure your sales team as a whole. Some companies measure gross profit while others measure total revenue. Be selective and opt for the metrics that are most meaningful for your company.

Here are a few more questions to answer to complete a basic sales assessment of your organization:

- Are the top-ten objections well understood, and is the sales team knowledgeable about how to deal with them?
- Do you have a clear plan for reaching multiple stakeholders with specific and relevant messaging in potential large accounts?
- Do you have specific plans in place for how to engage your top-ten accounts so that they continue as customers?
- Have you tracked and published sales activities by

sales rep and stack ranked them by revenue percentage of plan and by customer satisfaction metrics?

- Does your incentive compensation plan reward the behaviors most important to your business? Does it motivate your sales team in the right way?

As with the marketing assessment, by answering these questions, you can more easily identify gaps and opportunities within your organization.

CONCLUSION

———

Now that we have discussed strategy and execution, it's time to inspire your team to action.

Start with your leadership team, since they own the mission, vision, values, and business plan. Once they're all in agreement, they can each go and work with their individual teams on the execution of the agreed-upon plan.

Effective communication at all levels of your company is essential, because it keeps everyone moving in the same direction, toward a common goal. Aligning sales and marketing in the right way gives you the biggest opportunity to fuel growth.

Instead of sales and marketing being at loggerheads, they should be working in harmony, pulling in the same direction, to guide leads down a strategic and effective marketing and sales funnel that ultimately results in improved sales productivity and win rates.

ALIGNING MARKETING AND SALES TO YOUR GOALS

As you communicate with marketing and sales, it's important to remind everyone of your mission, vision, and values. From that foundation, you can delve into your business plans and what you want the company to achieve over the next year.

Just as important as sharing your goals is sharing your plan to reach your goals. At Chief Outsiders, we use a *Where Will Business Come From?* chart. It's very simple, but it gets the whole organization to work together to figure out answers to that question. Where will business come from for your organization? Existing customers? Future customers? Current products? Future products? The most risk comes from developing brand-new products for new markets, but if that is where you believe you will have the most growth, you need to develop a clear plan for how you can pursue the goal while still selling your current product to your existing customers.

If you set the goal to grow by 10 percent over the next year, you have to determine how you're going to get there. What strategies will you employ to achieve your goal?

Make sure you are clear on your strengths and where you stand compared to your competition. Collaborate. Get your teams to work together to formulate a strategy based on where you think you have the most opportunity for growth.

For some of your goals, you will find actionable ways to meet them. For example, you should have a time-based goal for lead follow-up. A company that follows up on a lead in forty-eight hours gets a very different result than a company that follows up within an hour. So how will you meet the goal you put in place? Perhaps you need sales reps more available for follow-up. Or maybe you need to hire a few more people for the sales team.

ASSESS AND RESPOND

Ultimately, you want to ask yourself, "Have we looked at every aspect of our business from a customer point of view?"

Today, take a step to gather the voice of your customer in one or more ways. Do your SWOT analysis, and choose one strength and weakness to activate against. As you move forward, decide how to edit your strategy for more effective execution and sustainable growth.

Choose the ideas in this book that resonate with you, and

put them to work. Be deliberate about your plan. Stop random acts of marketing!

If you're a CEO, VP of marketing, or VP of sales interested in looking more closely into your organization to find opportunities for growth in marketing and sales, I encourage you to reach out to me directly. Connect with me on LinkedIn or email me at khayward@chiefoutsiders. com. I would love to hear from you.

ACKNOWLEDGMENTS

This book is the culmination of a lifetime of meaningful relationships and experiences.

I would like to thank Cam Hyde, Gary Guthrie, Doug Laurie, Doug Lord, Rich Barton, Kevin Francis, and Pat Martin, who are some of the people associated with Xerox Canada who believed in me and helped support and guide me as I climbed the corporate ladder from sales representative to vice president. Xerox Canada provided an amazing environment for personal development, learning, and training.

To Kevin Francis and Keith Roberts, with whom, for over a decade, I shared the experience of "making payroll," building, buying, and selling a company. It was quite a journey. Keith, you taught me many things, but most of all, you taught me how to negotiate—a skill for which I am eternally grateful. Kevin, your values-based leadership, operational excellence, and incredible sense of humor got us through the dark days. I will always be appreciative of your personal friendship, support, and belief in me.

Art Saxby and Pete Hayes, who also believed in me and for whom I am forever grateful. You welcomed me into the best group of marketing executives, within one firm, that I could ever have imagined. To my Chief Outsiders family (especially the "Westies"). I have learned so much from you. My work has been incredibly fulfilling, and this is truly the best company I have ever been a part of. A very special thank you to Jay Dunn, one of the best e-commerce CMOs in the business, for editing my first draft and providing great suggestions and feedback on the content.

I want to thank my friend Rick Leckey, a Vistage chair, whose encouragement, support, and friendship have been kind and generous. Your deep and excellent questions always have me thinking about how to get out of my comfort zone and be the best version of myself.

I appreciate my Vistage chair and personal friend, Lance Descourouez—for your friendship, counsel, support, and collaboration.

To Cameron Herold, a fellow Canadian, who encouraged

me to write this book in the first place. You have been a source of guidance and inspiration as I made the transition from full-time CMO to the consulting world

I am grateful to Linda Jackson for helping me find just the right book title and to Rachel Gogos for your support and guidance in moments of indecision.

I am grateful to be grounded by five "bestie" girlfriends (Debby, Susan, Linda, Nancy, and Judy) from my early childhood. You keep me grounded, dreaming, and are my best cheerleaders.

Last, but most of all, to my husband, Rick, who has been my partner in life and has always encouraged me to be the best possible version of me, even when life was sort of crazy.

ABOUT THE AUTHOR

———

KAREN HAYWARD relocated to the United States after two decades at Xerox Canada. In her work as a sales executive, as a sales trainer, in HR operations, and as a VP for both sales and marketing organizations, she used her innate ability to drive alignment between an organization's sales and marketing functions to deliver breakthrough revenue. She is passionate about the need to follow the voice of the customer and is able to operationalize customer insights to effect product positioning, sales enablement, and lead generation programs. She now focuses on mid-market and high-growth companies, right-sizing the sales and marketing strategies learned from a world-class organization. For the past five years, she has worked as a CMO and managing partner with Chief Outsiders, consulting for mid-market companies, specifically those that started over ten years ago (not in the digital age) and have struggled to grow or would like to accelerate their growth.

Karen's industry marketing awards include a Demand-Gen Top 10 Award for "Using Sales and Marketing Automation to Fuel Corporate Growth" (2008—CenterBeam) and a Stevie Finalist recognition for Best Marketing Department from the American Business Awards. In 2004, Karen was named a Selling All-Star by *Selling* (a monthly publication of Institutional Investor).

Karen is a regular speaker with Tech-Canada, Vistage USA, and the COO Alliance. She has also been a featured speaker at Interop 2007, On24 Webcast on Lead Farming, and a guest lecturer at USC East Bay and USF. In 2010, Karen was recognized by CRN as one of the Power 100: The Most Powerful Women of the Channel for driving top-line revenue growth and revving up CenterBeam's social media program. Karen holds a bachelor of commerce from Concordia University in Montreal, Quebec, Canada.

CPSIA information can be obtained
at www.ICGtesting.com
Printed in the USA
BVHW031928130120
569403BV00001B/37/P

9 781544 502533